# Insights
# Into Gang Culture
# In Belize

# Insights Into Gang Culture In Belize

## Essays on Youth, Crime, and Violence

Nuri Muhammad

**Belize**
_____ **2015** _____

Reynolds Desktop Publishing
http://www.reynoldsdesktoppublishing.com
Belize

ISBN: 978-976-95563-3-1

Book Cover, typography, layout and graphic design by Reynolds Desktop Publishing

Photographs courtesy of:
- Janus Foundation
- The Observer Newspaper – Richard Merrill
- Sankufa Magazine

Contact the author (email): innadynamics@gmail.com

*With the name Allah, the Compassionate, the Merciful*

*This book is dedicated to all youth of Belize, especially those in difficult circumstances*

# Acknowledgement

I thank all those who have contributed in making this a better work than it would otherwise have been. Over the years I have had many who helped me with typing, proof-reading and other task which helped to prepare this manuscript for publication. Without your help turning this literary dream into a reality would have been far more difficult.

I also owe a debt of gratitude to my family and extended family for their support, especially my daughter, Thameenah, who engaged me in many conversations over the course of editing these essays to clarify my thoughts and impressions on this topic. Special thanks to my wife Sakinah, who have been beside me for many years, supporting and encouraging me to put my writings on this topic into a book.

Of course I could not have gained the insight into this unique culture unless the youth themselves, some who have died very violent death and others who are still living in extremely difficult circumstances, but more still who have turned their life around and are living productive lives and making their contribution to the development of Belize; had they not embraced me and allowed me access to their narrative I would not have had the passion to tell this story. For this I am truly grateful.

And finally, I must acknowledge G-d, for blessing me with life and guiding me to the path of Al Islam, a way of life that balances spirituality with reason and motivates its followers to service for humanity. As a practicing Muslim, all of my work with youth is a reflection of this deeply held conviction that I must make the world a better place than I found it.

# Table of Contents

# Foreword

Since Ross Kemp visited Belize in 2008 and teamed up with the police to see the other tragic side of Belize City's gang story, the 'phenomenon' that Nuri Muhammad describes in a series of essays has only escalated despite several attempts and interventions to curb it. Writing in a clear and revealing style Nuri has succeeded splendidly in treating readers to his reflections of gangs in Belize since 1992. Nuri displays an uncanny knowledge of gangs in Belize City, traditionally with their identifiable leadership, internal organization and wielding control, often in violent or other forms of illegal behavior, over territory especially in Southside Belize City.

Although the genesis of gangs in Belize can be traced to the early 1970s when, with the influence of the movie *The Wild Bunch* Belize had its first exposure to criminal street gang activities, the decades of the 1980s and the 1990s represented the training grounds for what was to become a 'phenomenon' indeed. The incidence of Belize becoming a transshipment route for drugs to the U.S.A. created a new breed of street gang dealers; while deportees helped to create bases of gangs claiming to be 'Crips' and 'Bloods' that introduced new sub-cultural behaviors among their associates.

While searching for reasons of *"how did a tranquil haven like Belize ever produce citizens of such cruelty and insanity?"* the author theorizes that early childhood impressions are the greatest influence on future criminal behavior; and concludes that *"the kind of criminal mind that we are seeing in Belize is more out of a moral and social disease affecting our society in general than out of individual pathology."* Juvenile crime in Belize is perpetuated directly by gangs, and Nuri bolsters this with references to the Crimes Commission of 1992, and provisions coming out of the Crime Control Acts of 1990 and

1993. This led him to further conclude that, in retrospect *"twenty-five years of implementing legislations, beefing up the police, expanding the courts and increasing the space in the prison were not enough to address the social and economic problems that contributed to this phenomenal growth in crime in our country."*

By covering twenty-seven thought-provoking sections, Nuri weaves his thoughts of gang profiles revealing that they operate in groups of ten to fifteen members consisting of mostly black males between ages fourteen and thirty years; coming from underprivileged or dysfunctional homes of a single parent; and comprising of school dropouts. Peer pressure, sibling involvement, poverty and limited job knowledge influence their behavior and create a national security concern as gang related shootings are responsible for most of the murders in Belize City. The impact of all this is a grave concern for the general safety of citizens, as well as the negative economic effect on tourism. Resorting to using the military term *"primary, low grade insurrection"* in one instance to describe gang activity in Belize City, Nuri reveals that the gang culture diminishes respect for the security forces' ability to maintain law and order. In effect then, in paralleling Belize with Iraq, Israel and even Mexico, he conjectures that *"Belizeans are gradually waking up to the reality that urban terrorism is now becoming a part of modern Belize."*

A very telling section of the book is titled "What Worked: First Gang Truce." This occurred in February of 1995, and as Nuri described it *"The Truce provided a window of opportunity to address this very volatile sector of the population which, heretofore, was dealt with only by the officers of the police, courts and prisons."* Called the "Bird's Isle Declaration" the Truce was signed by fourteen gangs, and was an effort to emphasize and utilize skills training for gang members, and curb the outright hostility among them. Supported fully by the Government, a very positive organization was created, named the Conscious Youth Development Program (C.Y.D.P.), which provided employment, counseling and education for former gang members.

Within most sections of the book the author is careful to suggest, and in effect point out, initiatives that have been put in place by the Ministry of Human Development and the Ministry of Education. These include the Youth for the Future, Youth Enhancement Academy, skills advocacy programs, and the Institute for Technical Vocational Education and Training. As the title of the book suggests **"Youth, Crime and Violence"** covers a broad expanse of the situation being faced in Belize and paints a landscape envisioning a heightened anxiety among the citizenry to cower in fear. The sub-title though: **"Insights on the Gang Culture in Belize"** conjures up a picture of young black males which are the core of gang activities, and the center of a gang culture.

Nuri is ever cognizant of the fact that to understand the 'phenomenon' of gangs in Belize, there is a need to study the gang members themselves. He does this admirably in reflecting on one such figure, George "Junie Balls" Mckenzie, a notorious gang leader who was killed gangster style in the streets of Belize City in August of 2007. Nuri did not perceive "Junie Balls" as *"a plastic or commercial rude boy"* but rather as a person who constantly experienced the full attention of the police because of his gang activity on North Side Belize City. His fate is exemplified in many youth who want to change their image, and who pay brutally for that decision.

Admitting that there is a dearth of statistical data with which to work, Nuri suggests that it is the responsibility of the

Department of Corrections at the Kolbe Foundation to gather profiles of offenders. The intervention programs like C.Y.D.P. and Youth for the Future have, by the author's admission, just scratched the surface of the gang problem. He advances in a section titled "Personality Disorder" that some youths who display symptoms of this have been helped at the Youth Enhancement Academy, where they have contributed to their own reconstruction for self-development.

Rehabilitation plays a large part in the youths apprehended, charged for drugs and shootings, and incarcerated at the Belize Central Prison, or at the National Youth Cadet Service Corps, or at the Youth Hostel. Here Nuri provides very tangible suggestions for specifically turning the prison into a training center, advancing that *"it has been proven through scientific research that where jobs and educational opportunities exist the crime rate goes down."* And again he addresses the present unproductive way of dealing with Belize's crime situation as needing to be proactive and systematic. *"We have to turn around this waste of scarce resources into the bottomless pit of the present prison situation, and revisit the concept of rehabilitation as a strategy of investment for increasing the productivity of these incarcerated youth rather than warehousing them as we are presently doing."*

As recently as May of 2013 two persons attached to the Bureau of Conflict and Stabilization Operations (C.S.O.), commented that despite another fragile gang truce in 2011, Belize had one of the world's highest homicide rates due mostly to gang violence. Working along with RESTORE Belize, C.S.O. established mediation programs, and with foreign funding is presently working to extend conflict mediation to every high school in Southside Belize City. This constitutes another intervention, one which Nuri most likely welcomes;

*Insights into Gang Culture in Belize*

but realizes that it will entail much more than mediation in our educational institutions to transform a phenomenon, which has become a crisis, into a workable solution. As the gang violence continues, albeit somewhat abated compared to ten years ago, Nuri boldly suggests *"a formula for the way forward to be considered by the Cabinet."* He advances that if there is established a Commission of Crime Eradication this body, operating in four phases, or 'quadrants' would control and eventually eliminate crime in Belize City.

Nuri Muhammad's diligently thought-out essays have been written over a twenty-year period, and only just now compiled to be revealed to readers. ***"Youth, Crime and Violence"*** is a document that is a timely, well researched and scholarly work Placed in its proper context among all the other social ills affecting Belize, there is no doubt that the subject matter will be very welcomed by the reading choices of our populace. This reviewer is confident that future topical events, hopefully in the positive, will prompt Nuri to add more revealing essays to complement his discourse.


Lawrence Vernon

# Introduction

Insights into Gang Culture are essays that cover the issue of gangs in Belize, especially as it relates to the rapid escalation of crime and violence in our society over the last twenty-five years. They provide an overview of the phenomenon of gangs especially in Belize City, but are not meant to be an exhaustive academic study even though we hope they will provide the basis for further discussion and research of this unique social problem.

These essays were written over the last twenty years starting in 1992, when some were published in the Amandala, Reporter, Belize Times, Guardian and the National Perspective newspapers. Timelines were left in some of the earlier articles to give a sense of the evolving process of this phenomenon that has become a compelling challenge to our development over the last two and a half decades. Relevant footnotes were also added from current studies to encourage further research.

All the essays look at what the presence of gangs in urban Belize means in the context of the other challenges we face as a society coming to grips with such issues as poverty, distributive justice, governance, race, tolerance, child abuse, and a wide range of other social issues challenging our development process.

They attempt to broaden the discussion on this subject from one of blaming "bad black boys" from dysfunctional families on the "Southside of Belize City", to include a discussion on the prevailing socio-economic conditions and the pervasive moral atmosphere that influences this culture of gangs in our society today.

While as a culture gangs are inclusive of both young males and females these essays focus mostly on the male aspect of this phenomenon. Over 99% of the prison population in Belize is male, and young black males particularly, are the main preoccupation of the criminal justice system. However, the increasing role of young females in the criminal justice system cannot be underscored and there is need for more research in the pivotal role that women have played in this unique subculture, as mothers, grandmothers, wives, girlfriends, sisters and daughters(1).

Again these essays focus only on young black males because they are at the core of gang activities in Belize and because they are also exhibiting other alarming social behaviors that have affected their development. While we have not focused on this phenomenon among the Mestizo and Maya youth, it is clear that some similar traits exist in these ethnic groups as well. It cannot be overlooked that while this phenomenon of gangs has spread country wide and affecting youths regardless of ethnicity, it is from among the young black males in the urban center of Belize City that this phenomenon had its origin in Belize.

The problem of gangs cannot be defined simply as 'bad black boys' who did not receive enough spanking in their early years and thus turned out to be wayward and lawless. The issue of gangs in Belize has to be understood as a culture, rather than news reports about youths who 'jack' and engage in warfare among themselves or even seen as contained in one section of Belize City or among one set of people.

In fact, the influence of the gang culture in Belize goes far beyond the so-called, 'Crips and Bloods', or 'Gaza and George Street'. Through the influence of language, fashion and personality types it has reached into the homes of ordinary

Belizean families, especially those with teenage boys. Many families have lost contact with their young boys who have become more attracted to peers outside the home than listening to what mommy and daddy have to say. Many parents are alarmed at their inability to reach their young boys of 14/16 years old unless they resort to threats and intimidations.

I also examine the antecedents of gangs in these commentaries. Where did this "thing" come from? Was it foreign in origin as some say, or was it homegrown? It is difficult for some to understand that it was both foreign and local in origin at the same time. It was foreign in the sense that the media images of the gangster in the 1980s and 1990s were the black youth of Los Angeles, New York or Jamaica; his gait, his stance, his mannerism and language formed the prototype that was made a global iconic figure through movies, (like, Colors and Menace 2 Society), music videos and the recording industry. However, while these images were foreign in style, there were socio-economic and historical conditions in urban Belize that provided the fertile environment for our own crop of gang activity.

In the late 1970s, after the Drug Enforcement Administration (DEA) had successfully disrupted the ganja trade in Jamaica, many of the traffickers and planters moved their operation to Belize, especially in the Orange Walk district. In the 1980s the "Belizean Breeze" became the premium marijuana replacing the famous Jamaican Blue Mountain senseimeon as the highest priced weed on the American/European market. Most of the "Breeze" was produced in the Orange Walk District. That brought a new dimension to crime in Belize. The D.E.A. successfully moved their eradication program from Jamaica to Belize and soon thereafter, the marijuana crops of Belize were destroyed by the aerial spraying of the germicide

Paraquat. However, despite the destruction of the marijuana trade in the mid-eighties, the trafficking network already established to ship the "Breeze" continued with a new product line: cocaine, coming from the Cali and Medellin cartels in Colombia. Belize had now entered a new era of crime, and youths were the pawns that were drawn into this new opportunity for them to attain instant wealth. So Belize had a fertile environment for its own form of gang activity.

When we examine the gang phenomenon in Belize today we see more than the imitation of a foreign culture, rather we see the creation of a sector of hardcore criminals with their own set of values and definitions of what society is all about and what means they will use to survive in a social environment they view as increasingly hostile and unfair. These are youths who were drawn into a powerful network of quick money and corruption in high places and it shattered their innocence of a civil and patriotic Belize. They lost hope and as a result became rebellious to the status quo.

What are the implications of this situation for the stability of our society in the years to come? We suggest that if the government does not take decisive steps now to intervene in pro-active ways with this sector in community-based programs, as well as rehabilitation initiatives within the prison system, we will end up going the way of Jamaica and other areas where this culture has become so ingrained and seemingly impossible to uproot.

But even today, there is still a disconnect between policy makers and the real work that must be done in youth transformation. Clearly the first step is an unequivocal commitment on the part of government to tackle the issue of youth development in a comprehensive manner; an expensive investment in human capital in its initial stages but one that will have untold value for dollar benefits in the long run. The problem is that the policy makers, like their counterparts in the rest of the Caribbean region, are shortsighted in respect to investment in a broad and comprehensive youth development policy. I hasten to say that it's not a result of any malfeasance on their part but just the lack of decisiveness by successive governments to tackle the issue and make the financial commitment to see the process all the way through. This journey requires a long-range strategy, one that will stretch beyond the life of any one-term government and therefore requires collaboration beyond political party lines.

It is also important to state in the beginning of this conversation that the majority of Belizean youth are law-abiding citizens and clearly the biggest challenge in front of them today is preparing themselves to meet the challenges of this increasingly sophisticated and technological world. As Belize evolves faster toward globalization and the decreasing importance of national boundaries as a criterion of power, our youth are challenged to develop their human potential to meet their counterparts, not only across the nation of Belize, but across the globe.

With the remarkable advancements in the areas of communication and transportation and the recently implemented Caribbean Single Market and Economy (C.S.M.E.), Belizean youths will be facing youths in Trinidad, Guyana and Barbados, instead of just Corozal vs. Belize City. Our small population is still manageable for investment in educational development of our youth, to guarantee that they will be captains of this ship named 'Belize' in the next twenty-five years, instead of only laborers and consumers.

But the inclusion of those who have become at risk for crime and violence will also remain a major part of our national challenge over the next twenty-five years. We cannot afford to leave them out of the process of transformation to productive citizenship. Our problem has been in understanding this sector and increasing our success at engaging them in life-changing productive activities.

A major part of these essays address issues affecting the community in general and especially families. If any short answer can be given to the question of why we have been overwhelmed by crime and violence and the growth of this marginalized sector of youth criminals it would be the breakdown of the family structure and by extension, the moral underpinning of the community.

Crime and violence are like opportunistic diseases that infect a body whose immune system is weakened. Just like the virus, H.I.V., which actually does not kill the patient, but so weakens the immune system that opportunistic diseases begin to infect the body, so too has Belize been infected with a virus-like condition that has so weakened the social immune system that the strength that once emboldened us as a society has become weakened, substantially, and as a consequence, we are seeing the infections of social diseases previously unknown to our society.

Despite these challenges, the road in front of us is still filled with opportunities for intervention but it will require determination by all of us to do something about improving the possibilities for these marginalized youth. It is our hope that these essays will leave you with a sense of optimism that successful intervention can be made with this neglected sector, and that when they are respected for their uniqueness, they are just as willing as any other citizen to make their contribution to the development process in Belize.

Finally, these essays were done in a narrative form and in a reflective mode. They are more an expression of concern and a sharing of experiences of one who had the opportunity to be close up with this sector of youth over the last thirty-five years. There is no attempt to impress the reader with an academic format with strict arguments and counter-arguments, and tedious data to prove a point, etc.; we leave that to those with the training and time to take that approach; ours is simply an echo of an urgent call that can be heard in all quarters of this society about the concerns for our youth, and especially those at risk.

So in the end, these ideas are mere food for thought, albeit, provocative. They are meant to stimulate further discussion and spur a pro-active movement, especially, by those with the power (government and N.G.Os) to curb this scourge of youth crime and violence and to use their efforts to help these youths to transform their lives and become productive citizens of Belize.

# Section I
# The Problem

## Chapter 1
## The Big Picture

### EARLY FAMILY INFLUENCE

When we take a close-up look at the so-called gang phenomenon in Belize, we find young men caught up in situations that are not entirely of their own making. Many are victims in a cycle of events they were born into. This does not excuse them from personal responsibility, but it forces us to look at the bigger picture of our social values and structures to see what circumstances created this phenomenon in the first place.

*Crime is an act of personal choice and an effective criminal justice system holds individuals accountable for their criminal behavior. Nevertheless, those who wish to prevent crime before it occurs cannot ignore the fact that the majority of people filling our prisons come from impoverished backgrounds and lack a formal education*(2).

Young men in Belize are vulnerable to crime. They often live in poverty; they are exposed to influences and images that raise their aspirations and purchasing desires beyond their means; they want to be providers yet their education or skills do not afford them the jobs that pay well. There are many young men in similar situations that have come together and formed groups. In a number of cases this leads to gang membership – a life of violence, crime, drug use and extreme risk-taking behavior follows(3).

While the sector of youth involved in hard-core gang activity in Belize is still comparatively small, the culture that goes along with it is wide and far-reaching. The so-called gang symbols, of clothes, language, walk, etc. are all symbols of power that many youths will identify with, and act out in their daily lives, even if they don't belong to a specific criminal gang. This is one of the reasons why the police, in their zeal to round up suspected gang members, often harass innocent youths who, because of their style and mannerism appear to fit the profile of the 'rude boy'.

Many children who grow up in single parent homes become healthy well-adjusted and successful adults. However, numerous studies in Belize and elsewhere have shown that there is a connection between lack of a father figure and problems such as delinquency and low academic achievement especially amongst male children(3).

The problem began in the home, or because of the absence of one. Many of these youths were deprived of a healthy, nurturing environment that every home should provide.

During childhood, most of the rapid growth of the physical, mental and emotional selves occurs. We begin to experience ourselves, and the world around us during childhood and the predominant aspects of our personalities are formed here. The events and persons that are impactful during childhood will strongly affect us throughout our lives and will largely define out responses to people and to life in general(3).

It is known that if there are too many emotionally traumatic experiences in the early development of a child's life that this will continue to affect that child psychologically until that trauma is reconciled; but if it is not reconciled it continues to persist in new sometimes distorted forms. What we see being acted out in the streets is a reflection of this trauma in its later stages referred to by some psychologists as, 'post-traumatic stress syndrome'.

Numerous studies have proved the relationships between childhood experiences and adverse behavior in later life – school drops-out, discipline problems, early sexual initiation, teen pregnancy, substance abuse, violent and risk taking behaviors are all said to be caused at least, in part, by dysfunctional family structures(3).

## ABANDONMENT BY FATHERS

Abandonment by fathers of their responsibility as caregivers is one of the major causes for the distorted images of manhood displayed by many young black males in the streets of Belize City today. Men who father children then abandon their responsibility to provide for those children materially and especially by their active presence, are a menace to the Belizean family structure and nowhere is this seen more than with the many delinquent males without a positive father figure in their early life. Many go on to learn the rules of manhood from the streets, the prison, and the distorted images projected on TV and the music/video industry; images that equate manhood with sexual prowess, money to spend, and the illusions of power by any means necessary.

This absence of a positive father/male image also affects young females but young males are especially affected because as males they are expected to be "a man", but without a close up, hands-on involvement of a man in his life, it is hard for that young male to be "a man." In some cases the biological father may be present, but his image in the eyes of his son may be that of an 'emasculated wimp' in a system that a younger generation perceives as needing more of an 'in your face' aggressiveness to survive.

This particularly happens when the conversation between father and son breaks down. From birth until he begins to 'smell himself', a boy is under the influence of his father in an absolutely obedient position but when that boy's transition begins in his adolescence years many fathers tend to remain at the 'do as I say...' level without adjusting to the new influences and information his son is coming in contact with as he matures.

While the boy is growing and transforming some fathers remain in the same old mindset failing to adjust their conversation to suit their maturing son. This breakdown in the conversation causes the boy to turn outside the home, usually to his peers, as his new source of self-identity. This disconnect between father and son in values is seen in many areas of conflict in families where boys are more attracted to street values than those he was raised with. Some parents feel that they have lost their sons to the influence of the streets.

## NO BLACK HEROS

But how did we get to this point of rebellion with our boys? Collectively, as black men we have not offered these young black males strong images of character for them to follow, we have left their 'hero formation' to the streets. This is not to say that such distinguished heroes or characters of distinction did not exist in Belizean history, but we have not done enough to keep these positive images of accomplished black Belizean males in front of our youth in our conversation with them.

All civilized societies celebrate their heroes for the sake of posterity of values and ethos. We have had many such heroes in Belize, but as 'Sefe' Coleman used to say, "Don't wait till the man dead to tell him he's good". The fact is we have had a problem with acknowledging each other's good works and contributions. We have left the space for black male heroes empty and barren of Belize's contribution to human development and civilization and examples of the endurance of the individual, despite challenges.

As black men, we have been so busy trying to make sure the other black man did not move out ahead of us and become a hero before we did, that we have developed the habit of tearing down and criticizing every little achievement that the next black man has made; in that process we have cancelled out all the possible black Belizean male heroes for our young boys to emulate. In a culture where every black man's achievements become 'lone rass', there can be no heroes for our young black boys to emulate. We have not made noise about or applauded each other's endeavors or achievements. Maybe we do so momentarily in sports and entertainment, but even that is not sustained for any length of time enough to reach "hero" status; other than that we do not publicly acknowledge each other's accomplishments. Andy Palacio had to be acknowledged outside in the international world before we realized the genius we had in our midst; and what do you say of Dr. Arlie Pitters or the maestro, Frances Reneau?

Just ask our boys who their heroes are and see whom they come up with! Then count how many of them are black Belizean men! More than likely they won't know about a Clifford Betson, or Cornelius "Pat" Chacho, Jaime Noguera, Telford Vernon, Charles Hyde, Horace Young, Godsman Ellis, Edny Cain, Wilhelm Arnold, C.L.B. Rogers, Edmund Martinez, or even Sgt. Hubert Vernon, who led the rebellion in 1919 and took over Belize town for forty-eight hours. Or even Samuel Haynes, Antonio Soberanes, Phillip Goldson, Leigh Richardson, or Albert Staine, and so many others who were trail blazers at a time when things were far more challenging in Belize than they are today.

Even today they will not know of the many present day black men of distinction in our midst, like Sherman Zuniga, Adolf Lucas, Dr. Kenrick Leslie, Dr. Joseph Palacio, Ambassador David Gibson, Evan X Hyde, Ambassador Bert Tucker, Eamon Courtney, Denzel Jenkins, Dickie Bradley, Rene Villanueva Sr., and the list goes on of the many potential heroes, potential motivational forces we have at our disposal; but because of this inherited crab syndrome we have become iconoclastic, killing every possible hero in sight.

The achievements of these black Belizean men and so many others like them are underscored and buried by our gutter-sniping habit of denying others like ourselves the honor and respect they deserve; not so much in social ceremonies where we give artificial accolades, but more in our daily conversations where our children listen to us and observe how little respect we really show to the achievements of other black men.

Let's face it; collectively, we blew it; our youths do not respect us! When we see them acting out their distorted perception of manhood in the streets of Belize City today, we really should look at it in a bigger context, and we should be willing to accept responsibility for not providing a culture of high esteem that told these youths who they were and where they came from.

## CULTURAL INFLUENCES

To understand the root of the problem, we also have to ask ourselves what kinds of cultural influences were impacting our youths during the years before our independence and the early years after, (1975- 1985). What was the state of our culture and the institutions that were to support it?

We did not extend to the Belizean youth a historical root to hold on to; his 'story', to define himself as a youth coming to maturity in modern Belize. Marcus Garvey said that a people without knowledge of their history, is like a tree without roots. From the very beginning of our so-called nationalist movement in the fifties we have maintained an argument about our history. During the seventies, just before independence, when we should have been promoting our own unique brand of Belizean nationalism and patriotism, incorporating the uniqueness of our history and multi-culture as a way of life and a stimulus for development, we were instead still caught up in arguing about the myth or non-myth of the Battle of St. George's Caye; a leftover from earlier days when the People's United Party (P.U.P.) challenged the colonial status quo by questioning the veracity of the legendary battle. Decades of failing to reconcile a united interpretation of that history has left our youths victims of shallow political arguments on both sides and that failure to resolve the difference in historical interpretation of the so-called Battle has remained a divisive wedge in our national consciousness, up to today. The youths don't know what to believe; and over time, they don't care.

Again in the seventies and eighties, when we should have been stimulating a culture of our own uniqueness in our diversity as a people, using culture as an instrument of development, we were instead interpreting culture as art and dance exhibitions, ethnic dishes, colonial architecture, mystical ruins, and other unproductive idiosyncrasies, all to the satisfaction of our supposed "tourist product". Today the mental space of our youths that should have been filled with love for Belize and Belizean heroes has been instead, influenced by North American television images of plastic heroes and an inordinate love for consumer goods. In consequence of our collective neglect, our young people have formed their own values drawing from the plastic images they see on television which, by the way, hitched a piggyback ride on our independence three decades ago, much like a master plan. In a way, we can see today's youth as the children of independence, but we can also see them as the product of thirty years of television.

We also have to ask ourselves about those social structures that were supposed to provide healthy stimuli for personal and social development of the individual, i.c. the family, the religious institutions, the schools, and the government. What has been the state of these in the last thirty years? Certainly the first three have declined in importance and impact while the latter has inherited a role that it finds it is unable to fulfill. We are now expecting from government what governments are incapable of fulfilling, given the nature of that institution. Responsibility for character development and implanting of values must go back to the first three institutions of family, religion and education. Government's role is to create an enabling environment that supports the existence of these three as character building institutions.

While our approach to dealing with youths in Belize must be multi-fold, two areas need to be emphasized: On the one hand we must address the social and economic conditions that affect the ability of a young person to reach their fullest potential as a Belizean citizen. At the same time we must build upon those initiatives that promote the character of citizenship, encouraging and insisting on productiveness and industry. Our young people need a healthy dose of patriotism; a sense of love and respect for Belize, which comes from a healthy love, and respect for one's self.

Clearly our local experience with youth, crime and violence are only the symptoms of a global social cancer that is affecting many other countries but it will not go away if our social intervention programs remain reactive. We must take the initiative and implement pro-active programs, based on our local circumstances designed to attract these derailed youth back to a course of self-development and national involvement. While this is a big job, it is entirely achievable. We are fortunate that we are experiencing a first generation gang crime problem, which can be reversed if we are decisive and concerted.

It is unfortunate that young people in Belize have no voice to lobby for better conditions for themselves as youths. More often than not, youth issues are presented through adult-run organizations and even when youths make decisions, those decisions are subject to the veto power of the adults in these organizations or government agencies.

Young people should be the center of the decision-making processes on those issues that effect change among them as youth, addressing their own problems and meeting the challenges of their own development. This should be the goal. Youth should provide the leadership and be facilitated by the institutional memory of those elders who should serve as their support. Even if they should fall short in achieving their objectives in the execution of projects they should be allowed the same space provided to others to learn from their mistakes. While some may have a dismal impression of the future of our youth, in fact, the situation for those of us on the ground is quite different. Many youths are engaged in addressing their issues and ready to work in partnership as long as their special and unique contribution is respected. Youths are ready to play their part in national development; it's up to us to give them their due respect.

Real and lasting change can only be effective if it is comprehensive enough to cover the whole subject and involves every one of us. Clearly government has the major role to play, but the onus for real change rests with all of us, the people of Belize.

# Chapter 2
# Born Criminals?

It is an undisputed fact that criminals in Belize have become increasingly barefaced and bold in their assaults on our society. This present dilemma has provoked a number of questions and concerns. How did a tranquil haven like Belize ever produce citizens of such cruelty and insanity? Were they born to be like that? What are the factors influencing criminal behavior in Belize? Is it the result of prevailing socio-economic or environmental conditions or are there biological factors that influence the individual criminal mind?

Research on the biological factors influencing the criminal is not new. Italian criminologist, Cesare Lombroso, in the nineteenth century, suggested that there were clear marks of degeneration that could be identified by studying the physical attributes or features of the criminal. This respected scientist came up with marks of degeneration that included "small ears, receding chins, crooked noses, thick lips, low foreheads", etc. all of which showed a person's predisposition to commit crimes.

In his scale of degeneration, the dark features of a person suggested that he was more inclined to be criminal than the person with the same features but of lighter complexion. The term "criminal type", was popularized during that period and referred to a "dark, shady character". It's not hard to see the obvious racial overtones in that supposedly scientific position, yet for many years, Lombroso's theory strongly influenced the Euro/American criminologist approach to detecting criminal behavior. In fact, today in Belize, there are still some people who believe they can spot criminals by looking at their faces.

So the question of whether a person's genetic make-up may be responsible for their committing crimes or acts of violence has been around for some time. As much as there are those who believe that genius derives from "good blood", there are also those who believe that evil and criminality is derived from "bad blood".

In the mid-1960s there was research done on the chromosomal composition of the person which found that the normal person possess the Y chromosome that accounts for his aggressiveness and an X chromosome from which he derives his gentleness; together they balance each other which accounts for normalcy, symbolized by XY, however, those with XYY chromosomal constitution were found to be more inclined to increased abnormal aggressive behavior.

The possible link between XYY chromosomal constitution and criminals first came to light in the sixties based on a study done by Dr. Patricia Jacobs, at the Western General Hospital in Edinburgh, Scotland, who published her findings on 197 mentally abnormal inmates undergoing treatment in a special security institution in that country(4). Dr. Jacobs's research seems to confirm that those inmates with the XYY chromosomal constitution had a history of violence and were more inclined to continue their uncontrollable aggressive behavior(4).

Of course, as with any chromosomal study, the above research does not conclude that genes are directly responsible for the end result of any person's behavior. Responding to that widely published research, Dr. Ashley Montagu, in 1964, wrote in "Chromosomes and Crime":

> Genes do not determine anything. They simply influence the morphological and physiological expression of traits. Heredity, then, is the expression, not of what is given in ones genes at conception, but of the reciprocal interaction between the inherited genes and environments to which they have been exposed(5).

Another consideration in this area of research into the biological roots of crime has been damaged to the fetal cortex of the brain as a result of birth complications. In a study of 41 murderers in the United Kingdom over a decade ago it was found that all of them displayed the same type of brain malfunction and were all prone to impulsive behavior. All this has led some researchers to the conclusion that damage to the actual brain function of criminals can be verified with tangible data. British researchers have seen that in cases of children who suffered birth complications and also maternal rejection, that both together affected a greater disposition to violence. Interestingly, this research found that separately they did not affect violence, but in those studied, the more violent children were found to be those who had suffered both birth complications and rejection.

Another interesting area of research had to do with hyperactive behavior, a syndrome that is very prevalent in the inner cities of the US among African American children, especially males, and can be seen increasing in schools in Belize City. Since these children, particularly if they are not treated, are at high risk for misbehavior, they are more likely to get involved in criminal behavior at some point. This research found that to the extent that a child is always getting into arguments and fights and becomes identified as "rude" or "bad" and that child's behavior becomes uncontrollable, and he perceives himself as radically different from other children around him and therefore the object of constant rebuking, is the extent to which the criminal mind of that child is being nurtured.

There is now enough research to verify that there are learning disorders like attention deficiency syndrome, (ads), and dyslexia and others that affect the psychological development of the child. Such children are faced with a handicap that is often misunderstood as a dysfunction, and can be wrongly diagnosed because of the lack of proper information. How many of those who end up in a life of crime started in a situation where their problems were misunderstood and therefore misdiagnosed by caregivers from the very beginning and therefore were beyond their capacity to overcome? Many of them were the problem learners in primary school, misunderstood and misdiagnosed by the staff and administration.

Again, from a physiological perspective that is backed up by scientific evidence researchers say that if there is one predominate attribute that stands out as distinguished from other factors it is that convicted criminals are overwhelmingly males. The greatest percentages of violent criminal offenders, world-wide, are males. This has lead scientists to look at high levels of the hormone, testosterone, as another biological factor in considering what drives the criminal mind.

Even though research on the biological influence on criminal behavior has gained respectability among some criminologists it is still not accepted in the courts, which hold that personal responsibility is the cornerstone of the legal system. Such research can also get out of hand. Imagine a time when scientists could predict by chemical analysis that a person was predisposed to crime. The argument could then be used by the defense that it was a chemical reaction in the brain that caused the defendant to commit the crime, therefore absolving him of personal responsibility.

Most current research in the area of criminology, however, leans more on the side of nurture than nature as the reason for criminal behavior. The strongest evidence points to the early childhood impressions as the greatest influence on future criminal behavior. It is in the early personality formations that dispositions are formed. British researchers followed thousands of adopted twins who were separated at birth over a thirty-year period and found that in most cases of criminal behavior, the adopted parent was also involved in crime.

Perhaps the most radical contributor to the predisposition of the criminal mind in Belize is poverty. Plato said, "Poverty has twins: crime and revolution". By poverty I do not mean only economic hard time. Surely, in Belize we have weathered the storm of economic hardship in the past and we never turned to crime. But this poverty I speak of is a culture of dependency that grows out of prolonged economic deprivation and comes when people begin to depend on hand outs, whether cash, goods or service for their survival. This is a poverty of the human spirit. This culture of poverty stifles initiative and dampens creativity and people begin to accept their social situation as fate. This kind of poverty influences the social environment and setting in which values that promote and condone criminal behavior are born. It also brings with it all the above ingredients which researchers say affect crime, such as birth complication, maternal rejection, abandonment, malnutrition, bad mentorship formations, the presence of hyperactive behavior which go unchecked, dyslexia, taken for "dumb", child abuse, and incest, all these and more go with the life of stress in Belize today caused by this culture of poverty which gives birth to the criminal mind.

The kind of criminal mind that we are seeing in Belize is more out of a moral and social disease affecting our society in general than out of individual pathology. What we have is a sickness in our society of which criminals are the statistical symptoms. This is not to suggest that some individuals with psychological malfunction cannot be diagnosed, using strict psycho, social and economic analysis, however; even these would verify that this culture of poverty is the common denominator that runs through 98% of the cases of criminal behavior.

# Chapter 3
# Patterns of Juvenile Crime in Belize

Crime is one of the major challenges facing Belize today. Its impact affects the quality of family life as well as the economic stability of the nation as a whole. Crime is a major preoccupation of the radio/television news and a regular front-page story in the weekly newspapers. Crime is the subject of tidbit conversations among friends, as well as the topic of talk shows. Its occurrence is national, regional and international. Crime is large, and has become an "established" part of modern life in Belize.

Our discussion in this essay is focused on juvenile crime and its impact on the frequency of crimes in Belize. 'Crime' can be defined simply as, "an act which is against the law," and 'juvenile', as a person who is "not old enough to be considered an adult." Therefore, "juvenile crimes", are those actions that are against the law that are committed by persons who are not old enough to be considered adults. Belize has a small population of a little over 350,000 people. It is estimated that two thirds of its population is less than 35 years; therefore, Belize is a nation with a young population. Over 70% of the prison population of 1,500 is under the age of 30 years; therefore, Belize's prison population is predominantly youth. Seventy nine percent of the prison population is serving sentences of less than one year, and 59% is serving sentences of less than 6 months. The majority of prison sentences is for drugs, and is served by those who could not pay the option of fines(1).

When it comes to crime in Belize, the age of adulthood is nebulous. Although, one is not adult enough to vote until 18, one can be sent to prison at 14, for up to 6 years for robbery.

There have even been cases of youth sentenced to prison at age 13 because it was felt that there were no alternatives to dealing with the nature of their criminal behavior and the requisite punishment.

An interesting observation when studying crime patterns in Belize is first to realize that crime is not a 'crime' because it is committed but because it is reported and therefore becomes a public issue. That means that a crime can occur, but because it was not reported, it has "not happened". Statistically we become aware of a crime because it is reported, investigated, and prosecuted. The media plays a significant role in the reporting process. If this process is not implemented then "actions which are against the law" can occur, but they "do not exist", or are not counted through the statistical data collection process of report, arrest, media, court, and prison records that we depend on to detect crime patterns and its effect on a community.

Keeping this in mind, we can then look at the frequency of reported crimes in the urban areas of the city and district towns as compared to non-urban and rural areas of the country. Because the urban areas have more police per citizen than the rural areas, the crime reporting and detection process is well established in the city when compared to the single policeman who has to police a wide area in the rural areas. People in rural areas may have complaints about dishonesty, domestic violence and incest and other actions that are against the law, but because of the lack of an established legal process in their surroundings they are forced to find other ways of dealing with their problems. In urban areas however, the process is well established and all the services are available to address complaints of citizens or reports of crime; therefore the reporting, investigative and prosecutorial process is in place. This discrepancy makes the incidences and patterns of crime in the two areas appear different.

Crime also has a direct link with the socio-economic issues affecting a society. The greater the economic disparity, the greater will be the incidence of crime. As the saying goes, "the rat will find the cheese".

> Poverty is not an excuse for crime, nor is crime the exclusive province of low income persons. But overall, countries with the highest ratio of poverty have the highest rates of crime....It does not follow that an increase in poverty will translate immediately into an increase in crime, however it does strongly imply that if overall poverty is reduced, then in the long run the amount of street crime associated with poverty will be reduced as well(2).

Because there is a relationship between poverty and crime, it is assumed that only the poor and not the rich commit most criminal acts. But as in the example of discrepancy in the urban and rural areas as cited above, the frequency of crime is not what has occurred but what is reported. A few years ago the Commissioner of Police acknowledged that very little of the Police Department's resources is allocated to "white collar and organized crimes", such as fraud, embezzlement, money laundering and other forms of sophisticated criminal activity; but such crimes are occurring with great frequency in Belize, although they are not recurrent in the nightly news.

The question of who handles the drug trade in Belize still remains unanswered. Is it the rich or the poor that comprise the network to facilitate the transshipment of drugs and arms through Belize? Such enterprises require an elaborate network of well-placed contacts. Yet in discussions about crime in Belize, the major focus immediately goes to those youths from West Street, Lake Independence and Port Loyola areas of Belize City, because they make the news headlines and statistically they comprise the arrest, court and prison records. They also constitute the most disruptive factor in the peace and stability of the social order, therefore they constitute Belize's "crime problem".

Most inmates in the Belize Central Prison are poor, young, black males from the urban areas; this gives the impression that most criminals are young black males. Statistically while this might be so, it is not because there is some biological degeneracy which makes these young black males more inclined to crime, but rather because of the above named factors, namely: (1) that crime has a socio-economic dynamic; (2) that more crimes occur than are reported, investigated, prosecuted and receive media attention in the urban areas; (3) that persons unable to pay the option of fines will be confined; (4) that the rich who commit crimes are not stigmatized as criminals and if caught have the legal resources to avoid imprisonment.

The Crimes Commission[8] in 1992 highlighted the causes for the rise of crime in Belize as being:

- Breakdown of family

- Poverty

- Drug abuse

- Migration

- Invasion of North America values through Television

- Structural weakness within the Police Department

Not much has changed during the last 20 years except that things have gotten worse. All the above have had a tremendous impact on the issue of youth crime and violence. From broken families or children who are raised without the assistance of both parents come youth who are more vulnerable to the negative peer pressures that affect juvenile delinquency. Research confirms that most youth in the Belize Prison system are from one-parent families. Most were raised without a strong, disciplined relationship with a father. Nowhere is the "missing father syndrome" more prevalent than in the prison population. Most youth in prison have a good on-going relationship with their mother, but rarely so with their father.

It is known that the strength of the community is the family. When the family structure is weak the community is affected. It is when the vital structure of family begins to deteriorate and fail to perform its proper function, especially regarding the children, that society must step in as a substitute or surrogate, to help the child to be nurtured, disciplined and when necessary, 'corrected'. In an ideal situation this is a normal function similar to the role that an extended family would play when there is hardship or difficulties in the birth family. However, when there is a widespread breakdown in the proper functioning of families in a community, the social institutions responsible for providing that kind of support become overwhelmed and they too begin to dysfunction.

The Child Care Center, Youth Hostel and Listowel Boys' Training School were three early attempts to address children in difficult circumstances in the 1950's, 1960's and 1970's. These institutions had commendable records of service in their early days but as the impact of the breakdown of our moral fortitude and the socio-economic issues came to bear on modern Belize in the 1980's and 1990's, it produced a new crop of delinquents and these institutions became less effective and in some cases totally ineffective. Research now shows that the ones now in prison were at one time in Listowel, the Youth Hostel and the Child Care Center(1). That would suggest that at every level of care, they fell through the cracks.

Statistics show that there are more males in prison than females. While this is true universally, wherever there are prisons, worldwide, it should not lead to the conclusion that there is no problem of crime among women. There was a 300% jump of women in Belize's prison, from 5 in 1997 to 15 in 2006. In the Youth Hostel, which houses both males and females, there is a dramatic increase of females in that institution. It is clear that while males are traditionally the most at risk for "reported" offending behavior, that young females are also entering the criminal justice system with more frequency(1).

The socio-economic conditions have changed in the last twenty-five years and this has had a devastating effect on family life in Belize and has resulted in more children ending up in institutional care. The breakdown of moral precepts that at one time governed the conscience of Belize was replaced by a new culture of, 'nobody can tell me what to do', and this has increased tensions in personal and social relationships. Social and moral obligations decreased, as everybody was looking out for their own.

It is clear that juvenile crime will remain a high priority on Belize's national agenda for some years to come. The fact that as a society, we waited too long before we began to address the challenge of intervention, prevention and rehabilitation of our youths involved with crime, that we have allowed a criminal culture to take root among many of our youths. This popular culture is region wide and most youth identify with it. The messages being sung or recited in dub, reggae and dancehall relate to every country in the region with its own values, language, dress, walk, and dance – an entire way of life. A culture, born in the ghetto and nurtured in the prisons, has spread to the nation through poetry, songs and dance hall music.

It is not easy to challenge this culture since it is a youth response to much of the hypocrisy and inconsistencies that they see in the status-quo culture. However, this bold challenge should not deter caregivers from recognizing the urgent need for help that these youths are crying out for. This help must take three key factors into consideration:

- The challenge to work with youths is more a vocation than 'just a job'. The task takes skill, but it also takes dedication and love, albeit, sometimes a tough love. The caregivers must have their head and heart in the right place.

- These issues surrounding youth, crime and violence have their roots deep in the history of our country, especially over the last twenty five years and are deeply interwoven in the very fabric of our value system. Therefore, whatever we do must be approached as a project in motion; a dynamic process, taking into consideration the many interrelated factors. Working with youths cannot be approached as a simple problem that can be solved at the end of a linear project or program.

- Finally, the stone, which the builders have continued to reject in this whole process are the youths themselves. They are the integral part of the problem and therefore must be the key to the solution. Give them respect and appreciation and watch how they will come up with "solutions," that will add to a more holistic and comprehensive approach to tackling the challenge of youth crime and violence in Belize today.

## Youth Department issues statement on gang violence

BELIZE CITY, Mon. Nov. 1

In the wake of the recent rise in gang violence in Belize City, the Youth Department has announced that they will be making a renewed initiative to bring together rival gang members to discuss ways to prevent further violence and a revocation of a life of crime by young gang members.

The Department has been working with former gang members to convince active gang members of the importance of a truce and promoting the idea of youths from rival gangs working together to improve social and economic conditions which affect all of their lives.

The Youth Department will also be seeking the counsel of Jim Brown's "Amer-I-Can" program in California, which has had remarkable success in bringing together rival Crips and Bloods in Los Angeles.

The Department is convinced that the incidents of violence in our streets by young people is only the tip of the iceberg of a deeper malady affecting the Belizean society. And that it will require more than punitive action against these young people to stop the spiral of violence which threatens the stability of the City.

The Department is also making an urgent appeal to concerned citizens who would like to volunteer their time to work with the Department in this campaign to stop the violence.

Interested persons are asked to contact the Youth Department at 18 Church Street or call telephone #73479.

Contact person: Nuri Muhammad, Director, Youth Department.

*Newspaper Clipping, 1994*

# Chapter 4
# Organized and Disorganized Crime in Belize

Crime is a multi-complex social phenomenon that cannot be treated simplistically without giving deep thought to the many factors that make up what we see daily on the TV news or weekend front pages. Today Belize is no different than so many other countries in our region and internationally who are dealing with the diverse manifestation of this scourge, called crime. This essay, at the expense of being labeled simplistic will attempt to look at two aspects of our crime situation in Belize and attempt to bring forward some of this writer's observations and suggestion for a way forward.

Crime has two manifestations in Belize, one organized, the other unorganized or disorganized. Let us look first at disorganized crime.

**Disorganized crime** patterns get the most attention collectively from the police, media, courts, prison and members of the public who are victims or who are drawn by the sensational circumstances of the reported cases. Disorganized crimes so much consume the public's attention that the very existence of organized crime often eludes public scrutiny.

The following are examples of disorganized crimes:

*Crimes of Opportunity* – Robbery, theft, drug trafficking, burglary, handling stolen goods. These crimes are also called economic crimes since they are committed to generate income. Crimes that are motivated by opportunity can sometimes become lethal and therefore result in assault, grievous harm or even manslaughter, but these are indirect results of these crimes since their primary motivation is generating income.

Crimes committed by those associated with gangs can also be placed in this category of crimes of opportunity. Very little real study has been done on gangs in Belize but an anecdotal review of what we have been seeing in the last ten to fifteen years will reveal that gangs, as the term is used in Belize, do not represent any organized or orchestrated criminal organization as we see in other countries. Instead, what we have are clusters of youth who have bonded for friendship and camaraderie and not for organized criminal activity.

*Insights into Gang Culture in Belize – The Problem*

Criminality with this group is incidental, and not purposeful. Despite the fact that crimes such as possession of illegal weapons, handling stolen goods, assaults, etc. may be common place in this group their raison d'être is not to commit these crimes but to hold to the bond of friendship and protection of their turf. While these so called gangs may exhibit some form of organized behavior at the street level, their activities are better described as disorganized crime. It is not until they begin to exhibit the organizational skills and ability to deliver a product through some armed protection, or get involved in the transshipment process with big facilitators, that they become categorized as organized criminals.

Gangs, therefore, have two categories, the local street youth who gather in groups for support of friendship and camaraderie, who may indirectly be involved in criminal activities, and another group of those who are directly involved in some part of the network of organized crime.

***Crimes of Passion*** – Murder, manslaughter, aggravated assault, maim, wounding, rape. These are crimes motivated by intent to cause aggravated harm in pursuit of individual passion or personal gain. This is a category of crime that many ordinary people who go over the edge emotionally and do terrible things, get involved in. People who commit these offenses are not normally described as 'criminal', until after they have actually committed the offence. Our culture has changed from one of tolerance and trust, to one of hostility and rage; it takes very little to enrage a person now-a-days. When passions, such as anger, jealousy, lust and revenge, are not controlled, they explode into various crimes of passion. Crimes of passion are a direct reflection of the moral climate of the society in which they occur.

**Domestic Crimes** – These crimes have many forms such as domestic violence, incest, abuse, neglect, abandonment. These crimes are usually covered by a veil of privacy and secrecy, and often go undetected. The staggering amount of incest cases surfacing in Belize today is a sad testimonial to the frequency of this depravity. Despite the recent attention given to this type of crime in Belize, they yet remain the hardest to detect and prosecute because of a code of silence.

**Moral Crimes** – Carnal knowledge, buggering, (unnatural acts), driving under the influence, drug abuse, and public nuisance. These are crimes that evoke a certain moral indignation because they reflect a person out of control and one who has fallen below the accepted moral expectations of civilized behavior.

Some criminal acts, though they fall into the category of disorganized crime, can have patterns of regularity that make them appear organized, for example, the recent exposure that there are rouge policemen using their skills to coordinate brazen robberies, even murder; but while these criminal acts can be individually organized, they remain in this category of disorganized crime because they lack a structured hierarchy which exist in all forms of organized crime, from the rudimentary to the complex. There are also patterns or modus operandi in some criminal behavior that can allow police to detect the 'signature' of certain criminals. While this reflects a degree of organization the use of the term organized crime as you will see below, takes on more than just being individually organized.

The reality of **organized crime** in Belize is more powerful than all the incidences of disorganized crimes put together. The power of organized crime has to do with the economic resources (cash) at the disposal of organized criminal activity.

Organized criminal activity happens at every level of a country like Belize and in every sector. Local operators are connected to national levels that are connected to regional and global operators. To be called organized an organization must be able to deliver their product in whatever form that product takes, i.e., service or kind. In organized crime it is not the size of organization that determines power but the ability to deliver the product or the expertise for the enterprise at the right time and place.

Whatever exists of organized crime in Belize occurs within the constructs of an international crime network. This multi trillion dollar industry has one product: organized criminal activity in all its multifaceted forms with one commodity as fuel: drugs. At the highest international level of the crime network the liquid cash produced by illegal sales becomes an important factor in the economic systems of the world.

Organized crime also occurs at the local level in the streets of Belize City, but even at this level organized crime differs from random acts of criminal activity. The same hierarchy of control exists and the importance of delivery of the product is as essential to the success of the enterprise as in the higher levels of organized crime. What differs is scope and magnitude but the central precept of delivering on the product remains the same. Organized crime at the street level has taken some serious hits recently with the deportation of high profile personalities but that has in no way brought organized crime at the street level in Belize to an end.

At the street level crime becomes organized when there is a market and a product to deliver. Getting the product to the market is the objective of the enterprise. The more expensive the delivery of the product, the more organized and lethal the criminal enterprise becomes. Organized groups, called facilitators, or gangs, can be found throughout the steps of the delivery system, from the planter/producer in Colombia (and elsewhere) and the countless middlemen that facilitate the product through the processes till its final delivery to the individual consumer in the United States, Canada or Europe. The enormity of the product increases the market value and keeps the cost high, which in turn keeps the organized criminal system in place.

Organized crime takes many forms but the two that are most prevalent to Belize is money laundering and drug running. The two go together since the billions of dollars in cash from day sales that come into the system yearly needs to be legitimized. Money laundering is the means to accomplish that; there is more liquid cash being washed in Belize than the average of us realize. That liquidity forms a major part of the informal economy of Belize.

Much of what happens in organized crime is above the heads of the average of us. Another aspect of the power of organized crime is its ability to fly below the radar of public scrutiny in the media, by-passing regulatory structures designed to detect them. Very rarely does a ring of organized criminals get busted in the Caribbean and if so, it is usually at the lowest level of an organization, which in most cases is expendable, while the real core of power always continues. Organized crime has rooted itself in the Caribbean. There is no way we can combat international organized crime in Belize without partnership with countries in CARICOM, Central America, Mexico, US and Canada. In fact, cooperation with the US is essential since that country has the greatest experience with organized crime and provides valuable resource in our own battle against organized crime. But we must sleep with our own eyes in these matters.

The so-called criminal element, those involved in what we refer to as disorganized crime, is a very small part of the total population, less than a quarter of a percent. The real problem is not the 1500 criminals locked up at the Central Prison, but the environment or culture that is producing those and many more criminal minds like them. Even if we locked up all the known criminals, in a short time we will have a new crop equal in number or more because this issue is only partially about the criminal an more fundamentally about the circumstances that produce the criminal personalities.

The only way to bring disorganized crime at the community level under control is to involve the Community with the Police in the management of crime. Modern society will never be completely free of crime; therefore, an environment must be engendered that bring crime to a minimum and controllable level. That can only be achieved when the Community and the Police are engaged in crime management strategies.

# Chapter 5
# Triangle of Injustice

The criminal culture in the Caribbean has experienced a phenomenal expansion over the last two decades. This growth has evoked many public outcries for harsher actions against all criminals throughout the region and Belize has been no exception. The gradual disappearance of what was once considered a climate of tranquility has sent some Caribbean governments to extremes in response to this national, regional and international crisis.

The sentiments go something like this:

"Why should we as a society tolerate any kind of criminal behavior as a normal reaction to social and economic pressures? After all, many of us had it tough and did not turn to crime, so why should we find excuses to justify why some people commit crimes? Let's get tough and serious and send a message to the criminal element that there will be no mercy: if you commit the crime you will do the time. Let's flog if we have to, and while we are at it, let's hang a few of them too".

These are some of the strong feelings expressed by citizens throughout the region regarding their security.

Government reacted swiftly when Belize experienced the impact of the expanding international drug trade of the late eighties and the resultant gang warfare on the streets of Belize City in the nineties. New laws were implemented. Both the P.U.P. and the United Democratic Party (U.D.P.) governments passed harsh legislation in an effort to show that they were responding to the rising crime problem. Enacting stringent legislation also had great public relations value especially internationally, since it gave foreign observers, especially from the tourist and investment market in the North, the message that Belize was "serious" about combating crime.

By the mid to the late 1980s, cocaine was passing through Belize and the whole crime scene had changed. Big money was passing through the streets and poor youths saw a chance to get out of poverty through the drug trade.

But to understand this volatile period you have to go back to the late 1970s when the D.E.A. had successfully destroyed the ganja trade in Jamaica and the traffickers and planters moved their operation to Belize, specifically, in the Orange

Walk district. In the early 1980s the "Belizean Breeze" became the premium marijuana replacing the famous Jamaican Blue Mountain senseamion as the highest priced weed on the U.S.A. market. Most of the "Breeze" was produced in that district and that brought a new dimension of criminal activity in Belize with the landing of small airplanes on the Northern Highway picking up planeloads of the "Breeze" bound for the U.S.A. The D.E.A. successfully moved their eradication program to Belize and soon after the marijuana crops of Belize were destroyed by the germicide, paraquat. But the trafficking continued with the new product: cocaine, coming from the Cali cartel in Colombia. Belize had entered a new era of crime and youths were the pawns that were drawn into this new opportunity to attain instant wealth.

By 1990 the P.U.P. passed what was dubbed the Crime Control Act I(6). The law was described as "draconian" by Dean Barrow of the Opposition U.D.P. leadership at the time. He accused the government of writing a law, "patterned after the Northern Ireland experience in dealing with the I.R.A. ... and the Jamaica experience with the Gun Court".

However, the same Opposition, after becoming the next U.D.P. government in 1993, expanded the provisions of that law with new amendments and was dubbed Crime Control Act II(6). Incidentally and interestingly, the same Solicitor General, Mr. Ghian Gandhi, drafted both revisions to the act one for the PUP, the other for the UDP. Obviously by 1994 the UDP government was faced with an expansion of the same rebellious youths involved in this dangerous street enterprise and saw it necessary to enact even stronger legislation to combat what they viewed as a threat to national security.

The youth issue that had fermented seven years earlier had escalated to a more complex situation of youth killing youth in the streets and a public that felt threatened and frightened and called on its government to do more to stop the scourge of escalating violence. This sentiment drove both the P.U.P. and U.D.P. governments to be draconian in their response to the immediacy of youth crime and violence and insuring legalistic justification "to get tough" was a small price to pay for what was viewed as a social epidemic at the time that needed the harshest measures to stamp out completely; so whatever legal measures were necessary would be put in place to stamp out this scourge. Hence when nearly a hundred suspected gang members were rounded up and corralled behind a barbed wire fence at the Militia Hall, in 1994, the public generally registered approval.

The bottom line was that while playing politics with the issue of crime may have been useful in the dramatics of the nightly news, weekend newspapers and daily talk shows, the serious business of achieving citizen security in Belize was really above party politics; and every government had to do whatever it viewed as necessary to achieve it.

## THE CRIMINAL JUSTICE SYSTEM

The criminal justice system is made up of the police, courts, and the prison. Its role within our constitution is to protect society by apprehending, convicting and punishing criminals who violate the laws. In an ideal world the theme of "justice" should be the guiding principle of a criminal justice system, but in the real world that "justice" is often compromised in the face of public outcry for tougher actions against criminals.

In an effort to stem the tide of an expanding criminal culture over the last twenty five years successive governments have enacted anti-crime legislations, strengthened the interdiction powers of the police, invested millions in equipment and vehicles, quickened the trial process to facilitate convictions, instituted mandatory sentencing, and expanded prison space. Ironically, when observed closely, these provisions, instead of providing the sense of security among the citizenry they were intended to, have inadvertently contributed to the creation of a criminal culture that continues to plague Belize.

The operation of these three institutions, police, courts and prison, within the criminal justice system, has inadvertently become part of what I call, a "triangle of injustice".

## POLICE OPERATIONS

One example of how that injustice is perpetuated is the operation of the police in their war on crime over the last two decades. This is not intended in any way to indict the police or to suggest that there was some conspiracy on their part in trying to perpetuate injustice upon these youths, but to examine the circumstances, to show a very distinct pattern of the injustice that has occurred.

Police work had to change in response to the rising incidences of crime and the shift to drugs, guns and gangs in the 1980s and 90s as the main occupation of police activities. As public pressure on the police grew, government put provisions in the law to make police work more effective. These provisions expanded the powers of the police and relaxed the due process of law guaranteed to every citizen by the constitution. This theoretically, was to allow the police to "catch the criminals" more effectively.

By relaxing constitutional "search and seizure" procedures, for example, the police were, theoretically, in a better position to apprehend the criminal, who may have been withholding some evidence, and would be otherwise protected by a constitutional right which says that there must be "reasonable cause" to justify a search.

By justifying the need to be 'tough on crime', the legislation relaxed a constitutional principle guaranteed to every citizen and gave the police the power to search whomever they suspected. In Ireland, many years ago, where this British police tactic had its origin, the search may have been for weapons of civil war, but in Belize, the search was for "anything incriminating".

This meant that the police had the power to stop anyone they suspected or could enter private property and interrogate the occupants if they suspected the presence of drugs or weapons. Emboldened by the law and public sentiments to get tough, the police saw themselves additionally empowered in their war against crime. Unfortunately, in their zeal to fight that war, thousands of youths entered the criminal justice system over the last two decades, sometimes for 'fine/confine' offences, which then began their journey through the revolving doors of the police, courts, and the prison system.

It is important to note that the demand for more officers motivated the recruitment drive to bring in more new officers, unfortunately, the low pay scale, coupled with the low entrance requirements, meant that the cadre of new police officers was in most cases, not much different than the gang youths they were pursuing. The training period at the Police Academy was also short, which resulted in officers entering the streets with very little knowledge of the science of policing therefore relying on the "way we do ting" approach of older officers in the field.

Clearly, the work of the police in Belize has been commendable in their war on crime; nevertheless, they have inadvertently become a part of that "triangle of injustice" that contributes to the criminal culture that now burdens Belize. In their front line war against the criminal element of Belize they have 'successfully' sent thousands of youths to prison; some well deserving, but many for minor offences that started their long journey through the criminal justice system.

## THE COURTS

For expediency in the courts, the new laws removed the discretionary powers of the magistrates/judges in determining sentences. Sentences were predetermined and magistrates were limited in their power to discriminate and examine extenuating circumstances that some cases may have presented. This resulted in some cases where young 13 and 14 year old first time offenders were sentenced to six years in prison for robbery.

Provisions were also made to quicken the trial process, since in the early 1990s the courts became clogged up with more youths because of the increased power of the police to arrest. There was a need to increase efficiency in convictions. The introduction of the Quick Trial Court in 1994 was set up to facilitate that process. Under the guise of assisting tourists that were robbed and had to leave the country, the court was set up to bring the culprit to trial and dispense with the case in a matter of hours rather than days or weeks or months, as was the usual. However, since its inception, only an insignificant amount of cases have been of tourist interest, yet this court was responsible for sending hundreds of youths to prison. After going into disuse for financial reasons, this Quick Trial Court was recently revived under another name.

Most important to note however, are the two most alarming aspects of the court procedures that contribute to this part of the 'triangle of injustice': one is the staggering amount of youths who do not have legal defense and the other are those who remain remanded, sometimes for years, while they await trial. They are serving a sentence before being convicted. Legal aid is only provided in capital cases; consequently, the result is hundreds of youths passing through the Magistrate's Courts without proper defense. Also, in sentencing where the option is 'fine or confine', most must defer to the latter, because of a lack of money.

Those who cannot afford to pay bail are remanded, sometimes for years, in the slow-grinding due process of law. All this before they are found guilty in a system that professes that you are "innocent until proven guilty". It does not take a constitutional lawyer to see that something is terribly wrong with a system that, at the end of the day, affords the rich a privilege that constitutionally belongs to every citizen.

## THE PRISON SYSTEM

The third institution that contributes to this 'triangle of injustice' is the prison system. According to one source we are paying approximately $5,000 per year for every one of the1500 inmates in prison. That works out to approximately six million dollars per year to run the prison. When you add to the above cost a guesstimate of about 50% of the police budget and about 70% of the court's budget that is also spent yearly in processing this same sector of youths, you get an idea of the astronomical cost of dealing with this certain sector of criminals rotating through the criminal justice system.

The cost of feeding, clothing, housing, supervising, providing medical needs, etc. for thousands of individuals, many of whom are in prison for 'fine/confine' offences, is not only a drain on Belize's scarce resource but also a waste of human resources. When one considers that by the time these youths enter prison (post primary school), government has already invested millions of dollars in free primary health care and education on them. Now, in the prime of their productive years, when they should begin paying back society through contributing to the tax base, they remain a burden not only to the government, but the entire society.

While monies would be well spent on protecting society from rapists, murderers, and violent individuals, the fact is most of Belize's prison population is made up of youths, many of them repeat offenders, who have less than a year remaining on their sentence and who were confined for what can be considered 'fine/confine' offences. Some are in prison for what is called "economic crimes", such as theft, robbery, burglary and drug trafficking.

If the increase harshness of prison punishment over the last two decades was effective then why is recidivism (returnee rate) in prison so high? It is estimated by prison officials that seven out of every ten inmates released from prison return within a year. Harsher punishment and longer sentences have succeeded in warehousing more convicts. Despite some success we have seen in the rehabilitative approach taken by Kolbe, the prison population continues to increase. Prison continues to be a "university of crime".

In retrospect, twenty-five years of implementing legislations, beefing up the police, expanding the courts and increasing the space in the prison were not enough to address the social and economic problems that contributed to this phenomenal growth in crime in our country.

While they represented an understandable reaction to a social crisis, their impact on the social problems that produced the crisis in the first place was not realized. In reacting to one set of problems (increased crime), another set of problems, (expanded criminal culture), was nurtured.

Those legal provisions took liberties with the constitutional rights of the accused; they made it easier to target a particular 'menace' that was plaguing the society (gangs and drugs). But in the process, they have also increased the amount of youths being processed through the criminal justice system, becoming worse, instead of better. With intent to do good, these provisions created a new set of problems.

These measures should have formed part of a more comprehensive approach to addressing the root causes for the criminal culture in Belize, part of which is a culture of poverty and a breakdown of the moral fabric of the society. The problem of crime, especially among our youth must be approached by a multi-prong strategy, which justifies the suppression of crime at the same time that it sets up a structure for rehabilitation and reentry of these individuals back into society. Aftercare services are also important to insure that all efforts at suppression do not continue to be the catalyst for creating more criminals.

# Movement of Youth Offenders Through Criminal Justice System (1997)

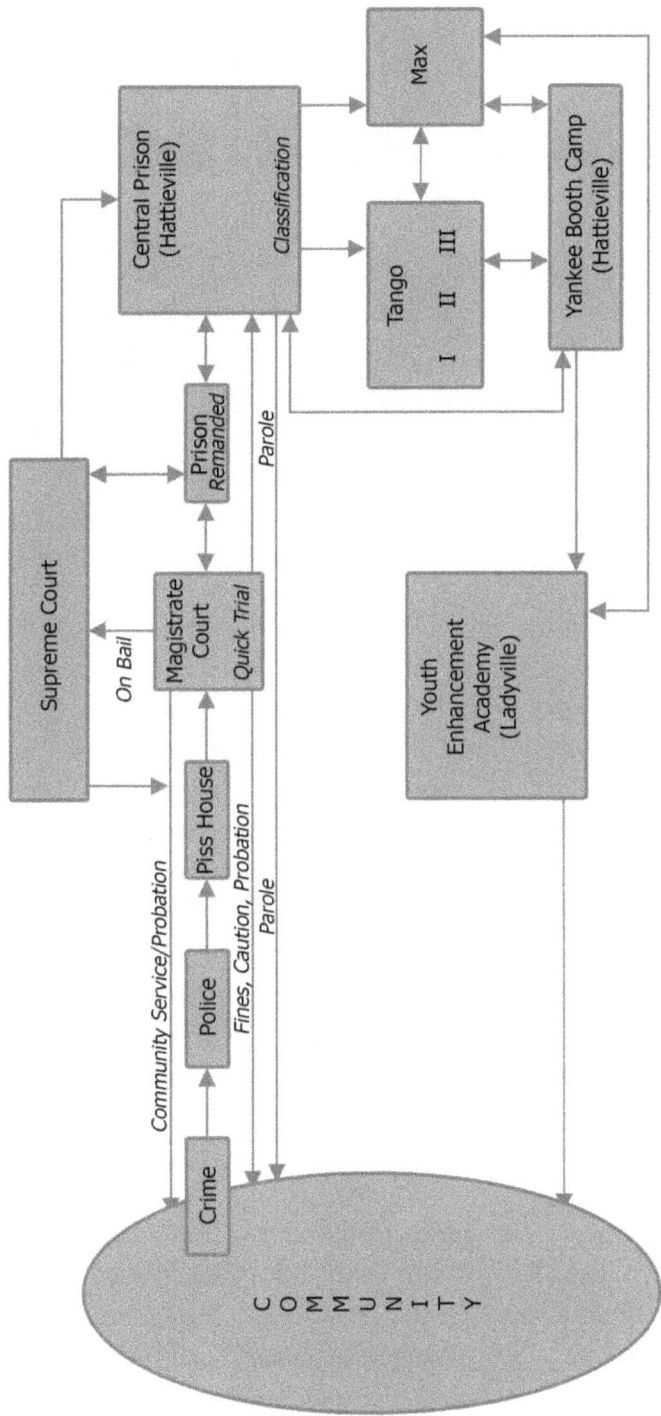

COMMUNITY

Crime — Police — Piss House — Magistrate Court — Supreme Court

Community Service/Probation

Fines, Caution, Probation

Parole

On Bail

Quick Trial

Prison Remanded

Central Prison (Hattieville)

Classification

Parole

Supreme Court

Max

Tango
I  II  III

Yankee Booth Camp (Hattieville)

Youth Enhancement Academy (Ladyville)

# Chapter 6
# Prison Reform

**"The degree of civilization in a society can be judged by entering its prison."(7)**

This is a brief overview of the current issues facing the prison system in Belize in 1997, to underscore the urgent need to reform that system. It is an accepted fact that the number one problem facing the prison system is overcrowding and under-staffing. There is no structured program of rehabilitation because the prison administration has been trying to cope with the overcrowded conditions. This has put the entire system in overdrive and has restricted reform.

How did the prison become so overcrowded? When did this increase begin? What were the social circumstances in Belize that gave rise to the prison population? From the 1950s to the 1970s, the prison population remained small and manageable. Prisoners were comprised of career criminals and some average citizens, mostly males, who were victims of circumstances. The average prisoner was between 20 and 30 years old. Crimes included theft, house breaking, wounding, grievous harm, and sometimes, crimes of passion. Police response to these criminal acts was effective and the court system proved adequate in dealing with all cases. The role of the prison at the end of this road of criminal justice was adequate in housing the convicted.

The old prison on Gabourel Lane, in Belize City, was originally built in the late 1800s to house eighty-five inmates. However, from the 1970s to the 1980s there began a slow but dramatic rise; doubling first, then tripling, then quadrupling its capacity with over four hundred inmates by the end of the 1980s.

From the mid 1980s to the mid 1990s, the nature of crime in Belize had changed, and what has significantly contributed to the change in the criminal justice system in the 1980s was government's response to crime. With the increase of drug-related crimes and its offspring, gang banging, there was a direct reaction on government's part. These direct reactions included improved and reinforced police surveillance, detection, and enforcement; instituting additional courts, expansions of additional prison space and a legal instrument dubbed the Crime Control Act(6). All these together dramatically changed the prison population of Belize.

What is the composition of the prison population today? Who are they? Where do they come from? Why are they in prison? The Hattieville Prison, as it is called, (actually the correct name is Belize Central Prison) which was built in 1993 to house five hundred, now holds an average of a thousand. The majority are youths who are not career criminals in the proper definition of that term, but because of their long arrest record, could be called, "repeat offenders". They are mostly young black males from the urban areas of the country. They are between 16 and 25 years old. They come from low-income areas and broken families; most didn't go to secondary school and many didn't finish primary school. They are poor and the reason why they are in prison is usually because they are poor, since, if they could afford it, more than likely they would not be in prison because they could have afforded the option of a fine or to provide a proper defense. Most of their crimes are drug-related, (more sales than use); acts of violence and hostility, and many of the crimes have an economic need tied to them, such as robbery, burglary, theft, handling stolen goods, etc.

The present prison population is made up of a significant number of recidivists or repeated offenders. In fact, what exists in Belize is not so much a 'crime wave', but rather an identifiable sector of youth who are revolving through the prison system, each time exiting worse than the last time they entered. Prison has become a university for crime.

Within our urban environment, we are producing more boys with no basic technical marketable skills, who are left to survive by any means necessary, using nothing more than the "smarts" they gain from the streets. These young, mostly black males have become the main clients of Belize's criminal justice system. The major preoccupation of that system today is the processing of these youth, from surveillance to arrest, detainment, trial and finally imprisonment. The system is clogged up with these youths.

Coincidentally, another noticeable phenomenon that is evident at the same time this is going on is the fact that more girls, disproportionately, go on to finish higher education. In fact, recent tertiary level graduations have had noticeably few young, black males. Our culture is beginning to echo something that we have seen for years in other Caribbean countries like Jamaica, Trinidad and also in the United States, that, among the criminal element, there is a disproportionate growth of young black males, while in the colleges and universities, there is a disproportionate reduction of the same.


## OUR CHALLENGE: THE TREATMENT

The challenge before us is enormous, almost overwhelming, but success is achievable if we change our present paradigm from prison to corrections, from punishment to treatment of offenders. The public at large and the professionals who work in corrections must make this change of mind; but most of all our policy makers must make it.

One change that will make a significant difference in managing the challenges within the prison system is classification of offenders. All inmates are not the same; their crimes are different and their temperament and backgrounds are different. At present inmates are all mixed together without distinction. Inmates should be classified in such a way that their treatment is based on how they are classified. For example, on a range of A, B, C and D, there are those who are A class, representing high risk inmates dangerous to themselves and others and therefore needing extreme security measures; and those classified as D class, representing extremely low risk and needing very little security and supervision.

With such a classification in place, it would mean that scarce resources would be distributed according to the greatest need. More security would be placed on A class inmates, while D class, especially youths, would be increasingly shifted into alternative treatment programs such as the Y.E.A.

Treatment of those offenders who can be treated should be one of the objectives of corrections. Many seem more interested in punishment than treatment, but they should remember that people are sent to prison as punishment, not for punishment; being in prison is already a huge punishment. Treatment may sound like being soft on offenders, but close observation of the process will reveal that leaving inmates without treatment (which is the status quo), is more costly, since it leaves the criminal element to continue to grow and expand. The treatment approach would change that, since it attempts to reverse that downward trend.

# Chapter 7
# Gangs in Jamaica: Lessons for Belize

Gang violence in Kingston, Jamaica, had become so rampant, that all businesses closed one day recently in protest against the violence that had overtaken parts of that city. Gang rivalry is said to be the major cause for the increase in violence. Over 75% of Jamaican law enforcement activity is directed towards combating crimes related to gang activities. The reality of gangs in Jamaica is large, and tells us the extent to which this type of social menace can break down the institutions of a society.

The root of gang activity in Jamaica goes back more than 50 years. Gangs are both a social and criminal phenomena in Jamaica. On the one hand, gang culture, rude boy culture, raga-muffin style, is a major cultural influence on the young, especially poor, marginalized youth. An expression of that same spirit of rebellion that produced the lyrics of Bob Marley and Peter Tosh, except today, it is tarnished by a heavy dose of nihilistic materialism, laced with sex and violence imported from the inner cities of the U.S.A.

On the other hand gangs represent an organized network of economic activity that stretches from Jamaica to London to New York, Los Angeles and Miami. The Jamaican "posse" has gained a reputation in underworld and law enforcement circles as a lethal force to be reckoned with. They have also gained the reputation as the gang which introduced crack cocaine to the streets of New York City. That same network however, has also represented economic survival for many who have not only enriched themselves but have turned some of their fortunes into community service for the deprived of the slums of Jamaica. To some Jamaicans the "posse" is viewed as a Robin Hood. Their criminal network has become a part of the informal economy on which many survive. The influence of the "posse" is so strong in certain communities that the police can only enter under heavy guard.

Gangs in Jamaica have also had a political influence since both political parties have used the gangs for political violence during political campaigns. It was reported that during the C.I.A.-backed plan to destabilize the Manley government in the 1970s, hundreds of high caliber weapons were mysteriously distributed to rival gangs who formed the street soldiers of both the People's National Party (P.N.P.) and the Jamaica Labour Party (J.L.P.)

The scenario in Jamaica holds many lessons for us in Belize. All the ingredients are present for the same kind of evolution in our gang culture if we lose sight of the critical and delicate nature of the problem that faces us now in 1995; and fail to support the effort now being taken to combat it through the GANG TRUCE. More important, the Jamaican scenario tells us that we must continue to invest our time and resources in combating this peculiar social phenomenon. If we do not nip gang activity in the bud in Belize, and seek to channel the energy of these youths to productive ends, we will be overwhelmed.

Like Jamaica, gangs in Belize have two manifestations: the rude boy rebel, and the gangster. The rude boy image is in many ways a fashion statement of the day. Dreadlocks, combat boots, dark shades, oversize clothes, sagging pants and slippers, are all "fashion statements". Most youths who wear these styles are into fashion, not violence. However, because these styles are associated with a violent street culture coupled with the pervasive "gangster rap", those who wear them are labeled "gang", when in fact they may have absolutely nothing to do with criminal activity.

The other manifestation of this culture is gangsterism, which may very well represent the greatest threat to our liberty in this city over the next few years. Gangsterism has a very fertile environment to grow in that part of our population that is comprised of youths under the age of seventeen, that same group that exhibits a 48% primary school dropout rate. In her research focusing on Belizean children back in 1993, Colleen Edwards sounded the alarm by referring to this segment of our society as: **CHILDREN IN ESPECIALLY DIFFICULT CIRCUMSTANCES**(8).

Not only do many of these youths suffer from the scourge of broken families and migration but many of them are suffocated by an ineffective and irrelevant educational system that does not cater to their special circumstances and leaves them ill prepared to deal with the challenges they meet after leaving school. An antiquated social service structure, and low moral and spiritual climate are also elements that contribute to that fertility. However, the most powerful of all influences is the present economic situation, which places a large sector of the population in displaced economic uncertainty. Youth unemployment in the urban areas is as high as 40%.

The absence of economic opportunity breeds anger and frustration even among law-abiding citizens: "a hungry man is an angry man". Those who resort to crime as a source of economic survival cannot be condoned but we must understand the circumstances that produced that kind of dysfunctional behavior. We are now recognizing that more than 40% of our youths are unemployed in Belize City. "Young people do not appear to have a clear sense of the skills levels necessary to obtain employment, creating a large gap between expectations and realities," says Edwards(8).

The court and prison records are telling us that we have reached a revolving door situation with a sector of our youth population, ages 14 to 21. These youths are black, male, and mostly from Belize City and Dangriga. They are in and out of the Police/Court/Prison system. They are charged with a variety of crimes from drugs to theft, robbery, grievous harm, attempted murder and murder. There is a core which some estimate as being several hundreds who are revolving through the system, who, in the last five years have been to prison at least twice, and have been detained dozens of times.

These youths are demonized by the media and castigated by the public but a close-up look at any one of these so-called hardcore gangsters would be quite revealing, if we took the time to care. Most of the time we blame the family situation for the behavior of these youths; mothers unfairly receive much of that blame. While it is true that they are a product of their home, the pressures that come from peers in school and in the streets today are equally as strong, if not sometimes stronger than the impact of the 'same ole same ole' style of parenting.

The fact is, what we have in Belize today are those same fertile conditions that germinate gang culture. If we do not want to go the way of Jamaica we still have the opportunity to avoid that path, but we must begin now to be proactive with interventions that will arrest the problem. We don't want to repeat the Jamaica scenario in Belize, so we must move decisively and with urgency to change direction.

# Chapter 8
# Myths about Gangs in Belize

The climate of healing and renewal among former gang bangers in Belize City between March and August of 1995 is testimony to how an innovative approach to solving a crime problem can bring results. Before the Birds Isle Declaration in February of 1995 the climate in Belize City was tense, the issue of Police Power, emboldened by the Crimes Control Act(6), and the description of almost every criminal incident as being "gang related" brought the public to a critical point of debate regarding the civil rights of the citizenry versus the need to bring the streets back under law and order. Many people seemed ready to write off this sector of youths as 'hopeless and good for nothing'.

Plato said: "Poverty is the mother of twins: crime and revolution." In the case of gangs in Belize we have a little of both. The rude boy culture is a budding rebellion and their survival instincts have become criminal. There are those who will argue that they grew up poor and never turned to crime or rebellion in early Belize; while this may be true what we face today is a different set of circumstances than those tamer days in Belize. In fact, what we have with gang activity in Belize could be described in military terms as "primary or low grade insurrection." The existence of the gang culture erodes respect for authority and undermines the ability of the security forces to maintain law and order in certain sections of the urban areas. This form of instability can lead to increased problems for security forces to maintain citizen security among the population in general. The very security of the social system is threatened if these elements are not confronted in their early stages with decisive interventions.

To understand the phenomenon of gangs in Belize, we have to study the gang members themselves; we need to bite into some statistical data on the nature of the problem. Unfortunately we have no such system to gather information on these youths besides arrest records and court documents. A system needs to be in place at the Department of Corrections (Kolbe) that can gather a psycho/social and economic profile of offenders. From this data can come some kind of statistical profile of the gang problem.

But even without that, there are some outstanding features that almost make statistical verification unnecessary. For example, it's primarily a "black thing," even though you will find its impact on other ethnic groups, like the signs of the Salvadorian gang, M13; it's an "urban thing," even though you will find pockets in the rural areas; it's a "poor thing", even though you will find "rich boys" identifying with it; it's a "youth thing,'" even though one or two OGs in their 30s and 40s are present; it's primarily an "unskilled, undereducated and unemployed thing," even though there are the skilled, educated and employed involved who take advantage of the vulnerable and desperate poor.

Because we lack this verifiable data there are some myths about gangs in Belize, partly created by media perceptions, some foreign and some local.

- **Gangs make enough money to give each gang member plenty of money.**

The facts are different. Of the fourteen active gangs in Belize City in 1995, most were comprised of youths who are poor, unskilled and unemployed. These youths are part of the marginalized class whose only power is the illusive vote every five years. They hustle any way they can, like most people who find themselves in an unemployed state. If these youths had occupation of their time on a daily basis in education, employment or sports, they would not be involved in criminal activity. Those who are involved in criminal activity do so on a "need" basis and not as a permanent occupation. While some gang members use "jacking" as a regular means of earning quick cash, most will work a steady job if they had one.

- ***Gangs control plenty of weapons on the streets.***

Clearly it does not take hundreds of lethal weapons to terrorize the public. The availability of a few weapons, especially grenades, is enough to do the same. The Chinese proverb holds true: "kill one, terrorize ten thousand". So a few weapons on the streets is enough to create fear and threaten citizen security. However, to suggest that gangs have a special armory of weapons that they use to war on each other and on the public in general is false. The fact is that weapons, including lethal ones, are rampant in the streets of Belize City and available to anyone determined to get them.

- ***Gang members are hardened criminals, tough, mean, and cruel.***

To survive the streets of Belize City today young males require certain toughness, as they go through their "rites of passage." There was a time in Belize when being detained by the police or worst, going to prison, was one of the worst things that could happen to your reputation, but today, among some youths, there is a certain degree of heroism in being able to survive the "pisshouse". But, if you meet most of these youths on a one-on-one basis, they are just children, albeit, in some cases, dangerous ones. These are hardened criminals by circumstances rather than by nature.

- ***Gangs are tightly-knit organizations with structure and discipline and they run the city.***

The facts are that gangs are loosely knit with a crude organizational structure, but there is leadership, which sometimes rests with more than one. To suggest that they control the city is an attempt to set these youths up to think they control something that they don't in fact control. What illusive control that does exist is over other gangs afraid to confront their enemies' power. However, what is important to realize is that given time, this crude structure will develop into a more sophisticated operation, as it has in places like Jamaica and Los Angeles. The beginning of any organization is movement, action and combustion, and all those elements are present in gangs in Belize, even if in an unorganized state. Over time, as the stakes increase and the money gets bigger, leadership will evolve out of the disorganization to give direction to this combustion and form organized enterprises in crime.

- ***Gangs are the main perpetrators of crime in Belize.***

Media hype has helped to create the language that made blaming gangs for all criminal activity in Belize City easy. Every crack head that snatches a chain or every robbery committed has been blamed on the result of gangs in Belize. The mindset that gangs are responsible for most crimes in Belize makes it easy to direct all criminal activities to this one phenomenon but the reality is that crime takes place in every sector of the society and gangs are not responsible for the majority of criminal incidences.

- ***Gangs are the tourist industry's main problem.***

This is another one of the areas that the gangs get the most blame. Even though there has never been one incident of a 'gang-related' tourist crime, the gangs are generically blamed as one of the problems affecting tourism. While it is true that headlines about "gang wars" can negatively affect the tourist market, the truth of the matter is that the major victims of gang violence are the youths in poor neighborhoods and not the tourists. Recent incidents of attacks on tourists have been from bandits from Guatemala and that has become a serious matter for the tourist industry; but again the gang or ghetto youth was not responsible for this alarm from the tourist industry.

# Chapter 9
# Urban Terrorism?

Is there terrorism in Belize? After years of watching this distant phenomenon in Iraq, Israel and even Mexico, from the comforts of our televisions, Belizeans are gradually waking up to the reality that urban terrorism is now becoming a part of modern Belize. This is real. It is obvious that the latest grenade explosion has taken center stage and we are currently in a necessary reactionary mode as we pursue these weapons of mass destruction; but there are some points that we must consider.

While the last three grenade incidents have resurfaced the existence of these weapons on the streets the fact is that these weapons have been out there for nearly three years. And according to sources, besides grenades, there are more lethal weapons on the streets. It is obvious that the intelligence is lacking in locating these grenades and this can be traced back to a number of factors, one of which is the lack of adequate resources to match the task at hand. Clearly, there is a need for more technical support but there is also need for large sums of cash to be used to effectively gain street intelligence.

All this and more should rightfully come from the British who must take moral, and some say, legal responsibility for the loss of the twenty four grenades in the first place. They should treat this matter with the importance and urgency it deserves, and by now should have provided all the necessary technical resources, including hard cash, to break this case. Anything else is tantamount to Belize being treated with impunity by the British government.

I agree with Godfrey Smith's comment in his newsletter, Flashpoint, that the British should be compelled to pay compensation to the families affected by these explosions. There is precedence for this in international law if this case were ever to be brought to the International Court of Justice, but of course we will never get our case that far. What I mean is that in principle the British as manufacturers of those weapons, which were brought into Belize through the British military for military use, is primarily responsible. In addition, they were lost due to their lack of security. They must take more than "moral responsibility". All this would appear to be a strong case in our favor for the international jurist.

In launching the recent truce the Prime Minister commented that: "This is perhaps the number one problem we are facing as a society, certainly in terms of Belize City..." Therefore he used his highest office to register how urgently the government views this situation in Belize City. But the grenade explosion brought the short lived truce to an end. This latest effort at a truce was government's attempt to recapture the same vibes from the first C.Y.D.P. experience, but this is a different time and those involved in this latest effort should realize that. The dynamics of gang activity in Belize is completely different today and the grenade incident was a wakeup call to that reality.

The "Truce" which was given high profile media exposure is seeking to capture an opportunity similar to what existed in February of 1995 when all the 14 active gangs in Belize City came together to put an end to violence and death caused by gang rivalry. That historical event took place on February 18, 1995, when a peace declaration called the "Bird's Isle Declaration," signed by all gang representatives and also signed by the then Minister of National Security and Deputy Prime Minister, Dean Barrow. But there are some fundamental elements missing from this latest effort, most important is that a truce cannot work without the youth gang members themselves owning it and having direct input in the process. After all, it is they who have to sustain the truce. There should be some kind of Council or representative body of the gang leaders themselves with one of them becoming the "voice of the truce". A government led truce will not last, as the grenade incident shows.

The first truce had youth leaders who told their own story to the community through the media. They formed themselves into a community-based organization (CBO), made up of members from previously rival gangs. There were ongoing rivalries among them but they put those conflicts on hold and supported the truce. So there would never have been an incident like a grenade explosion soon after a truce. The record shows that there were no gang related incidents for the first year of truce.

# Section II
# What Worked

## Chapter 10
## First Gang Truce

The first Gang Truce signed on February 18, 1995, was a historical declaration to stop the violence that, up to that time, had brought Belize City to the brink of a crisis. While the Truce was not a panacea to stop all forms of crime, it made a significant dent in a peculiar type of crime that had plagued the city since its inception in the late 1980s. The Truce provided a window of opportunity to address this very volatile sector of the population which, heretofore, was dealt with only by the officers of the police, courts and prisons.

Unlike Jamaica that had experienced gangs since the fifties, gang violence in Belize had only become a serious crime problem since the late eighties, as reflected by the Crime Control and Criminal Justice Act of 1990 and its revision in 1994. These legal instruments represented government's response to the community's outcry over this scourge, and had the elimination of gangs as its objective. But it was not until the Gang Truce of 1995, that any significant progress was seen in the attempt to control this problem. Police statistics verify that gang violence went down significantly in Belize City during the first nine months of the Truce.

The Truce was something that gang members themselves wanted. It was something that all sides wanted, but none was willing to make the first step toward peace. It had to be agreed by all, unanimously, before it could work. Thus, on February 18th, 1995, when every active gang in Belize City was represented at Bird's Isle for the historic declaration, it became a Universal Truce. Representatives of all fourteen active gangs in Belize City signed the Declaration of Peace, called the "Bird's Isle Declaration." The declaration, among other things resolved to: **"stop gang violence; work to heal the wounds of rivalry; improve relations with the police; and improve chances of a fuller life."** The emphasis was on life skills training, and developing the marketable skills of former gang members.

*Deputy Prime Minister, Hon. Dean Barrow (R) during a Press Conference in which he announced the convening of the Peace Summit.*

*Deputy Prime Minister, Dean Barrow, in 1995, giving government's commitment to support the truce.*

What was also historic about the Truce of 1995 was the fact that it represented the government of the day going out on a limb in an experiment with a most vulnerable sector of the society. For the Deputy Prime Minister, Dean Barrow to, in effect, put his political career on the line and enter into a participatory process with former gang members -- a marginalized sector of the population -- and attempt an innovative approach to addressing a problem that previously had been dealt with only with police power, was historic indeed. Belize was the first in the Caribbean and Central

*Insights into Gang Culture in Belize – What Worked*

American region, where similar problems exist, to venture into such an experiment and had many observable positive instances to attest to the success of this social experiment.

*Ex-gang members join their colurs as a symbol of peace*

Historic truce on February 19, 1995 when all gangs in Belize City met at Bird's Isle to sign the Peace Declaration.

Youth from rival gangs relax during break from work on the Infrastructure Project

# Bird's Isle Declaration

**We the undersigned,** in the presence of our peers and the rest of the Nation of Belize, do hereby declare that:

**Whereas** gang violence has become a scourge to Belize, threatening the lives of our citizens, especially the young, and

**Whereas** gang violence has tarnished the image of Belize as a tranquil haven in the heart of the Caribbean and Central America, and

**Whereas** gang violence has created a climate that threatens the tourist industry and job creation for our people, and

**Whereas** gang violence has created an atmosphere where some of our youths live divided against one another in open hostility and fear, and

**Whereas** gang violence has prevented our young people from moving freely throughout the city, without fear of harm or harassment, and

**Whereas** gang violence threatens to disrupt our schools' recreation and sporting events, and

**Whereas** gang violence has resulted in many youths being shot, chopped, stabbed, beaten up or killed, leaving parents, relatives and friends in grief and frustration, and

**Whereas** gang violence has resulted in many youths crowding the courts and prison system, and living in constant conflict with the police,

**Be it Resolved:**

1. **That** we call an immediate end to gang violence;

2. **That** we commit ourselves to work together to heal the wounds and spiritual scares caused by gang rivalry;

3. **That** we work to discourage youths, especially the very young, from getting involved in negative gang activities.

4. **That** with the assistance of the Government, the Private Sector, the NGO's and the Religious Communities, we strive to improve our chances for a fuller life with emphasis on developing our marketable skills.

5. **That** we work with the Police Department to improve relations.

**Signed, sealed and delivered by us, the undersigned, this 18th day of February, nineteen hundred and ninety five, in Belize City at Bird's Isle:**

| | |
|---|---|
| _____ Ghost Town Crips | _____ Backa Town Bloods |
| _____ Hoover Crips | _____ BlackScorpion Posse |
| _____ Plum Tree ~~Bloods~~ | _____ Kraal Road Crips |
| _____ P.I.V. | _____ Kick Down Fence Bloods |
| _____ Lynch Mob Crips | _____ Witness |
| | _____ Witness |

*The Original Bird's Isle Declaration*

The C.Y.D.P. was created to facilitate the process of re-entering and re-engaging these high risk youths back into society by providing counseling, employment, social and educational opportunities for these former gang members. A steering committee consisting of 16 citizens from the private and public sectors, as well as the N.G.Os and religious sectors was appointed to monitor and advise on programs implemented by a Secretariat, the body responsible for managing the day to day affairs of the program.

*Work on the Infrastructure Project was a major job opportunity.*

During the period of the Truce, which lasted over a year, all 14 active gangs in Belize City gave their support. They abided by the Truce through the respect that they showed to each other and the improved communication with the Police, which prior to that time did not exist. Of course, there were incidents of violence caused by personal rivalries; however during the period of the Truce those actions were not classified as gang related, as was the practice before the Truce. As a result of the Truce those who had no communication, and whose sole focus over the previous years was eliminating each other, started to relate to their common issues as opposed to seeing each other as 'the problem'. They started to participate on small projects with collective goals that benefited themselves as a group.

*Chester Norales (Coolie), one of the youngest youth benefitting from the CYPD project*

The primary objective of the C.Y.D.P. was to maintain the historic Truce and to occupy the energies of these youths in productive activities such as education, employment, counseling and life skills training. For over a year of the Truce there were no organized bands of youths killing each other, as was the case over the previous years. To this extent we can say the work of the C.Y.D.P. was effective. However, in the other area of its mission, that of occupying the youths in productive activities, the Program did experience some weakness in its delivery.

The Secretariat saw its mission as a team, comprised of players and coaches. The players were the former gang members and the coaching staff was the coordinators of the program. The program focused on internal and external/outreach aspects of the problem of gangs in Belize. The internal focus provided services such as counseling, referrals, follow-ups, training and building ownership for the process. A lot of time was spent in fostering relationships among former rivals. The external outreach focused on community relations, the employment provided by the side

*Insights into Gang Culture in Belize – What Worked*

walk building project, reentry into school, enterprise development, and direct street-based conflict resolution when the need arose.

The Truce was managed in the first instance by a team comprising of Sharon Palacio, Edward Boaster and Nuri Muhammad out of a Secretariat located on King and Tigris Streets in Belize City. Later Lauren Burgess joined the staff. The major preoccupation of the Secretariat was building "ownership" for the program among the former gang members. This was particularly challenging because the mindset of most of the youth in the

Jason Alvarez, proud to *be a part of CYDP*

beginning was, "how much money can I get out of this?" instead of, "how can I use this opportunity provided by the Truce to better my situation". The objective of the Secretariat, therefore, was to get the youths to understand that the Truce represented an opportunity for them to stop the violence and focus on their self-development as well as to get involved in the national development process as an organized group.

The Secretariat also started a Council with representatives from all the gangs. This Council was established to provide a forum to discuss their problems and to settle their conflicts peacefully. The Council had the task of moving the youths from 'gang mentality' to 'organization mentality' and taking responsibility for the outcome of the Truce and building ownership. This group, while a good idea, never made real progress. The discipline required to sit in weekly meetings to deliberate and then to follow-up on decisions was perhaps too ambitious a plan to expect of these youths who were just slowly coming to trust a system they felt, previously alienated from. So the Council became more a forum for discussion of issues of rivalry and concerns about police harassment.

The C.Y.D.P. also offered educational opportunities for former gang members who entered the Center for Employment Training (C.E.T.), and another group who attended remedial classes at the Lake Independence Methodist School. It also organized an effective school intervention program where former gang members who had experienced the dread of gang life went into the schools to discourage young students away from the lure of gang life. This program was nationwide and was supported by most secondary schools and a number of primary schools.

The program gave many former gang members like Anthony "Trigger" Atherly, Cleon "Tush" Smith, Arthur Young, Anthony O'Conner, George "Junie Balls" McKenzie, Victor "Scorpion" Logan, Paddy Meighan, Ursula Smith, Dennis Rhaburn, Timmy Stamp, Evalee Cadle, and so many others, a forum to speak to youths on the dangers of street life. This was a very effective program, because even though many of the presenters were still caught up in that life they were condemning, they were still very forceful in convincing youths that this is not the road you want to travel.

The main contributor to the weakness of C.Y.D.P. was the lack of resources. It was not decided in the beginning of the initiative that this would be a long term strategy; rather C.Y.D.P. was a knee-jerk reaction to something that nobody realized would work beyond a few months. But now there was an opening for greater possibilities, but the committed resources would be a necessity. The real challenge was not only holding the Truce but also ensuring that the resources would be made available to sustain the program long enough to see real results. It was not possible to realize real change among these youths without a long range plan of action that is resourced to do sustainable work. C.Y.D.P. was developing the vehicle to deliver that service when resources began to dry up.

Another area that contributed to the weakness of C.Y.D.P. was the absence of coordination in its activities. Activities were isolated and not tied to each other in any overall plan of action with clearly outlined objectives. Because the primary objective of the program was maintaining the Truce and keeping these black youths from killing each

*A carpenter makes his final inspection of the forms before cement is poured.*

other, most of its activities were centered on resolving conflicts and building confidence and ownership for the process.

# Gang Situation in Belize

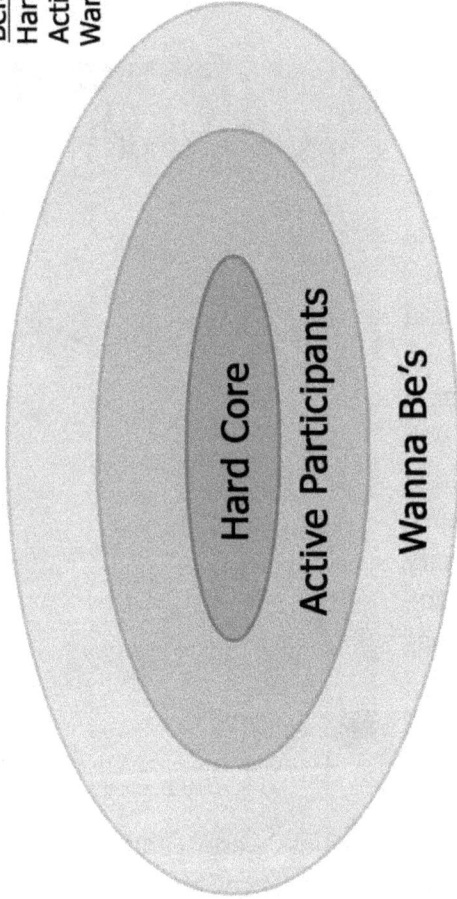

| Before CYDP | |
|---|---|
| Hard Core | 300 |
| Active Participants | 500 |
| Wanna Be's | 2500 |
| | 3300 |

**Non-Criminal Activities**
Hang-out Together - dance, other events
Dress Alike - colors
Sharing and Supporting Each Other
Plays Sports Together

**Criminal Activities**
Robbery/Other Property Crimes - economic enterprise
Drug Dealing - economic enterprise
Intimidation - keeping control
Violent Conflict/Flash Points - with rivals

# Memorandum

To:     Mr. Roy Bowen, Permanent Secretary, and Ministry of Human
        Resources
From:   Nuri Muhammad, Director, Youth Enhancement Academy
Date:   December 4, 1998

Re:     CYDP FORWARD

This memo is in response to your request that I make some recommendations to your Ministry on the way forward for CYDP.
After consultation with members of The Steering Committee, CYDP staff, and concerned citizens in general, it has become increasingly clear that there is a unique role for CYDP in the way forward to national development.

Clearly, the unique characteristics of the target group it is serving makes CYDP an important frontline intervention programme for moving pro-actively in addressing the needs of this sector nationally. The question that still remains is what role it will play within the Ministry of Human Resources in implementing this service and will the required resources be made available.

With this is mind the following suggestions are presented for consideration:

- **That CYDP become a unit within the Ministry with responsibility for coordinating programmes related to the specific target group, nationally,**
- **That CYDP becomes the Ministry's representative in co-operation with the newly formed Juvenile Unit in the Police Department for ongoing early intervention to resolve conflicts,**
- **That Ministry should take responsibility for facilitating continuing educational and training opportunities for increase employability of the target group.**
- **In co-operation with the Youth Start Plan, CYDP can facilitate the development of entrepreneurial training with the target group,**
- **Providing training through CYDP for persons in both the public sector and other agencies who need effective skills in dealing with this sector,**
- **Co-coordinating an anti-violence campaign within the schools nationally carried out by CYDP.**

*C.Y.D.P. going forward*

# Chapter 11
# Youth Hostel, Youth Enhancement Academy (YEA) and Youth Cadet Corps

What is the difference between the services offered by the Youth Hostel, YEA and the Cadet Corps?

To understand the difference it is important to first understand the levels of delinquency among our youth and those requiring institutional care. For the sake of this article, we look at juvenile delinquency in Belize at the following levels.

## LEVEL ONE

At this level the child or young person had difficulty at home. The parent (s) cannot manage or control the child's behavior. Usually the home environment is unstable and *the child needs temporary institutionalized care and supervision.*

The child, usually between the ages of 8 and 13, is not yet a threat to society and can attend regular schooling.

The Princess Royal Youth Hostel was created in the early sixties to target this population. This institution is governed by The Child Welfare Act and is not designed to be for punishment, but rather *to provide a nurturing environment with specialized care.*

However, because there has been no non-prison alternative program for youth at other levels of delinquency, the Hostel has had to cater to clients who they were not designed to treat.

At present, Hostels' clients are between the ages of 8 and 18 and are both male and female. These youth attend regular schooling and engage in regular community activities but reside at the Hostel.

The Youth Hostel offers skill training, personal development, recreation and sporting activities, counseling, community service and opportunities for spiritual development. These clients are referred to the Hostel either by their parents or by magistrates upon the advice of The Human Development Department.

## LEVEL TWO

The second level of delinquency refers *to youth who are becoming a menace to society.* Their behavior is not only inappropriate and unacceptable but borders on anti-social and sometimes criminal behavior.

They 'Hang Out' on the streets are unemployed, engage in petty crimes, and have minor contact with the law or with the criminal justice system. They are not yet hardened criminals but if their behavior goes unchecked and unsupervised, these youth can begin to commit serious crimes. They are unusually between the ages of 14 and 21.

**The National Youth cadet Service Corps** is targeting these youth, some of who are presently at The Youth Hostel, which does not have the capacity to adequately address the needs of level two delinquencies.

They Youth Cadet Corps will be a one-year residential program, which will include a six-week intensive boot camp period. During this period, the cadets will undergo a structured, highly disciplined phase, designed to strip them from their negative habits and help them build the positive character traits required to be successful in the remainder of the program. The program will include training in marketing skills, community service, counseling and an aftercare component that will lend support to the cadet for six months after he/she leaves the program. *The focus of this program will be on reintegration of the youth back into the community as a productive citizen* and not to extend his reliance on continued institutional welfare.

## LEVEL THREE

The delinquents have jumped from engaging in petty crimes to more serious offences such as assault, drug trafficking or even murder. These are *youths who entered into the criminal justice system by virtue of the nature of their offence*, but, however, are still not seasoned criminals. Many first or second offenders that are young and show signs of being rehabilitated if put in the right environment.

**YEA** is designed to deal with level three delinquents who have been sentenced to prison. It is a facility designed *to separate young offenders from more seasoned adult offenders at The Hattie Ville Prison.* YEA is designed to be a strict boot camp type program that focuses on character development, vocational training and community service with a view of preparing the offender to return into the community. This intervention would prevent his becoming a level four delinquent.

## LEVEL FOUR

These are delinquents whose behavior has become too uncontrollable to be treated in any of the afore-mentioned institutions. These are youths whose offending behavior require imprisonment in a more security focused environment such as Hattie Ville, even though, all is not lost for this level of delinquents. In the duration of their sentence they can still access opportunities for rehabilitation and possibility of Parole after serving at least half of their time. These delinquents can still be assisted by support structures within the community such as halfway houses and other aftercare services.

# Chapter 12
# An Overview of Some Aspects of Rehabilitation within the Department Of Corrections

In order for a structured rehabilitation program to exist within the Belize Department of Corrections (B.D.O.C.) three major factors must be taken into consideration:

- The Administration of the institution, i.e., its management of personnel, accounts, stores, staff training, deployment of resources, etc.

- Custody and Control: the security of the institution and the control of the movement of all inmates.

- Rehabilitation - the establishment of structured rehabilitation programs in the institution.

- The first factor is the administration of the institution which entails the overall management and responsibility for accounts, stores personnel, etc. Staff morale affects the effective operation of an institution.

- The second factor is 'custody and control', that is, maintaining a complete control over the environment of the institution to ensure that all those who are sent there as convicted persons will serve their time without any possibility of escape up until the time they are released back into the society. When an institution is not controlled and the custody aspect of the institution is not secured then the third goal of rehabilitation will always be problematic.

- Generally the concept of rehabilitation has been applied to any activity that attempts to reform the inmate: to challenge him to change his lifestyle while in the institution by providing him with access to programs and opportunities for him to grow in skills; to build capacity; to prepare him to make a change from his criminal lifestyle to the life of a productive citizen. In general terms, activities within a prison, whether it is religious, educational or any form of training are considered activities of rehabilitation. However, while these programs are an important factor within any institution if they are not structured their impact is lessened and is less capable of being quantified. What is missing in the Belize Department of Corrections is a structured rehabilitation program that takes the inmate through a process that starts at entry into the institution; one that can be monitored and in fact encouraged.

To do that requires a scientific approach to this aspect of rehabilitation. What is needed is a rehabilitation plan of action to be instituted within the B.D.O.C., which will incorporate and streamline all the existing programs and add to them additional programs and opportunities which will come from cooperation with agencies within government (i.e. Ministry of Education, Ministry of Human Development, Department of Community Rehabilitation, etc.) and N.G.Os (i.e. Faith and

*Insights into Gang Culture in Belize – What Worked*

Justice Commission, Lions Club, Rotary Club, Society for the Promotion of Education and Research, etc.) This corporation network will provide the opportunity for expanded programs available under the umbrella of rehabilitation.

## ADMINISTRATIVE STRUCTURE

In order for any rehabilitation plan of action to be effective there are some necessary administrative structures that must be put in place. They are the following:

**Risk/Needs Assessment:** It is important to put in place, immediately, the risk/needs-assessment profile of each inmate, those who are already within the institution and those who are coming in. At present an intake record, which contains basic information for each inmate including his name address, basic family background and information on his criminal record is used. What is missing from this information is a risk/needs-assessment or psycho/social profile of the inmate, information that will help in assessing the rehabilitation needs of that inmate within the institution. An inmate should be repeatedly assessed throughout his time in the institution to determine his progression or regression throughout his incarceration. Rehabilitation programs should be structured so that those who are best prepared in certain areas to take advantage of certain types of programming should be channeled in that area.

**Rehabilitation Unit:** There will be need to invest in a well-trained Rehabilitation Unit made up of officers who are already in the system. They will be correctional officers but, specifically identified as rehabilitative officers, will have to be those officers who understand clearly the role of these rehabilitated activities, and are therefore given the additional training to ensure that they are effective in their work, of monitoring, participating and in fact conducting some of these rehabilitative activities.

**Income Generating:** Any income generated by inmate labor will be divided in thirds. One third goes to general revenue for the up-keep of the prison, which should be highlighted publicly. Another third goes to a Credit Union account, which the inmate will not have access to until he leaves the institution. If he has a family only the immediate relative has access to that account. The final third goes into a Restitution Fund. This Fund is where victims are able to claim for the return of what they lost by way of property or some other form of compensation. This Fund can be managed by a community based Victim Support N.G.O.

**Victim Awareness:** A missing link within many rehabilitative programs is insufficient time spent on sensitizing inmates to the pain and anguish they cause to their victims. True reform begins when an inmate acknowledges the wrong he has done and makes a commitment not to repeat that behavior. We need to enhance inmates realizing that they have harmed their victim and they express some form of regret for what they have done. This can only be done when these inmates meet face to face with victims of their crimes.

**Networking with Voluntary Groups:** It is important to enhance the already existing relationship with the voluntary groups that come into the institution to assist with program delivery. These groups include N.G.Os and religious groups but they also include groups like the National Drug Abuse Control Council (N.D.A.C.C.) and other government agencies. These groups must be given an orientation of the standard procedures and the rehabilitation objectives of the institution. A degree of strategic planning is important to ensure that the

*Insights into Gang Culture in Belize – What Worked*

best deployments of rehabilitated activities are available for the inmate population and that it's not only to a certain chosen few. Voluntary groups, which include religious groups, must be encouraged to expand their 'care' beyond proselytizing to faith based counseling and other cognitive skills development activity like values clarification.

**Networking with Agencies Abroad:** It is important that the B.D.O.C. network with other correctional agencies abroad that have similar challenges to what we face in Belize. We are in a position to access technology and other resources and share experiences, and have exchanges between correctional and rehabilitation officers from our programs with others within the region, especially in the Caribbean, Central America, Cuba and taking advantage especially of our access to the United States and England.

## AREAS OF REHABILITATIVE ACTIVITIES

**Vocational Training:** A variety of vocational skills can be provided with the cooperation of the C.E.T. and other voluntary groups that come in to help structure vocational training opportunities. Necessary funds should be provided to build an area where this training will take place within the facility. A sizable amount of inmates will be involved in vocational training daily. We should have no less than a hundred inmates per day involved in some form of this type of vocational training, i.e. construction skills, furniture making and repair, plumbing, electrical, mechanic, etc.

**Agriculture:** Inmates should be involved in agricultural activities that will lead to some form of production i.e. eggs or vegetables or other things that can be marketed to hospitals, and hotels. We have to get the private sector involved in this project. A private sector person should be hired for the management position. Agricultural activities should serve as a training opportunity.

**Adult Education:** Classes where inmates are actually sitting at a desk in a classroom situation doing the kind of structured work by teachers in a structured and disciplined way towards passing very specific exams. They will have training through literacy, innumeracy, and communication skills development programs.

**Life Management Skills:** Life Management skills development includes a variety of programs that will help inmates to better manage their lives. Help will come from N.G.Os to provide enhancement type programs to assist inmates in their cognitive skills, that is self-esteem, self-awareness, critical thinking, areas that will assist the inmate in that aspect of his self-development.

**Outside Team Work:** Another area of activity will be outside assigned teamwork. This is for more skilled inmates who are going out of the institution for specific work. As pointed out previously those assignments outside of the institution should have a cost attached to them. There should be a clear accounting of the value of the inmate labor. Some of the benefits of this area of activity are:

- Society gains by reduced labor cost to public projects – value for dollar

- Inmates gain in skill training

- A Restitution Fund is replenished by one third of inmate remuneration

- General revenues of the B.D.O.C. gains one third

- A credit union account is given another one third

**Merit/Demerit System:** The merit and demerit system is based on the 'snake and ladder' concept; that there will be opportunities within the institutions and through these rehabilitated activities the inmate has the opportunity to climb the ladder. These opportunities to climb the ladder involve his being in training, in education or some other form of activity that he is partaking in and is being monitored. But he must also be aware that he could also put his head in the snake's mouth by violating the rules of the institution therefore ending up with the loss of opportunities. This culture must be established within the institution.

**Limited Resources:** Another important point of concern is how the limited resources for rehabilitation will be deployed. It is not possible at the beginning of this program to offer rehabilitative opportunities to all the inmates in the institution so a sizeable amount of the inmate population will still be basically confined to cells and be involved in limited activities. However, there are still opportunities for those who are locked down on a routine basis to be able to come out to specific programs such as religious and other development programs. Expand reading opportunities with access to reading material in the cells. The audio system can also be expanded in use to include training by audiotapes.

## KEEPING HOPE ALIVE

These innovative activities should create a different atmosphere within the prison because a missing element within the prison today is hope. These programs will provide that sense of hope for the inmate that genuinely wants the opportunity to change his life. For those who want to stay in their cell and rot, the choice is theirs.

It is important that the public relation of this rehabilitation initiative be handled very carefully because that injection of hope into this end of the society seems to be the opposite of what is expected from this sector. Most people expect that prison is a dreadful place where there is hopelessness and despair. However, it's important that society realizes from the very start that this is not a 'pet and powder' approach but a very strict and stern approach to corrections. What has been missing from the prison over the last decade, and perhaps has never existed in the prison except perhaps in the very early days, is a structured rehabilitation program. We have simply been warehousing these people, the majority of them being young black men, who have been degenerating and becoming worse than when they came into the prison system.

This initiative should not be looked upon as any attempt to go soft on criminals. It will be a stern, corrective and structured program of rehabilitative activities that will be monitored on a daily basis to insure that goals are being met. This structured approach will offer opportunities for inmates to gain structure and discipline in their lives, to build their character around some form of ethic and values, so that in that sustained environment they, perhaps, can get a grip on their lives and return to society better than how they came in.

# Chapter 13
# YEA Making a Difference

On August 1, 1997 the Youth Enhancement Academy (Y.E.A.) began its operation at Price Barracks in Ladyville, as an rehabilitation focused, correctional program for first-time youth offenders. As part of a series of reform within the B.D.O.C. over the last year, the institution was set up as a treatment program for youth offenders who were just beginning their contact with the prison system. One year later, a number of achievements have been realized. This came about as a result of the hard work of the B.D.O.C., including inmates, the support of government and the private sector, as well as that of a number of people in the broader community.

The primary objective of the Y.E.A. is to cut the recidivism rate of young offenders. Seventy-three youths have been released since the program started, and thus far, the records indicate that only nine youths have returned to prison with new offences. Prison records show that over the last ten years, starting in 1986, seven of every ten inmates returned to prison, sometimes months after being released. The prison population has grown over 300% from over 300 in 1988, to over 1000 today – most of whom are repeat offenders. The early results from Y.E.A. indicate that given an opportunity for change some inmates will take it.

Research indicates that the first 60 to 90 days of re-entry to the community is a difficult process for the average inmate. He is faced with many personal and social hurdles that he has to overcome with little or no support. According to criminologists, the three things that a former inmate needs to survive in the community during this critical time are a job, family support, and a strong set of moral beliefs. It is not hard to see that what the former inmate requires to survive is also what the average citizen needs to survive and stay on a straight course in life. Y.E.A. has tried to prepare these youths with the kind of values they need to meet the challenges of the real world.

The refurbishment of the old Price Barracks has gone from a run down and gutted state, to a renewed landmark of distinction on the Northern Highway. This was accomplished with very little resources. Although the support from government and the private sector was critical, it was the hard work of the Hattieville prison inmates who were skilled in carpentry, electrical, masonry, and common labor. Under the direction of prison officers they transformed the location into an operational barracks. This reconstruction work continues involving the youth of Y.E.A.

The Academy has processed eight intakes, each comprising of approximately 30 youths The six-week orientation program include foot drills, fatigue, muster parades, camp improvements and preparing the youths for what they will face during the rest of the program. After passing through this rigorous six-week period, they move on to academic and vocational training as well as life skills development. While over 200 inmates have already passed through this process, Y.E.A. has maintained an average population of approximately 130 young people.

There is an atmosphere of productivity at Y.E.A. Each week's activity is divided into four areas namely: education, vocational training, life management skills development and camp improvement. All daily programs are clearly defined, and are scheduled with outlined objectives. The entire day is filled with productive activities.

Education includes academic classes in primary subjects to improve basic competency skills. Presently two volunteer teachers do a splendid job of managing large classes. They are Mrs. B. Kingston-Smith, a retired Belizean teacher, and Ms. Jeanna Goemart, a retired American teacher. However, there are some adaptations that are needed to facilitate the learning process because the youths serve various lengths of sentences, so the academic program requires some flexibility.

Our educational focus has been more on teaching the youth how to learn and how to apply what they learn. With the help of the retired teachers, these young people are getting a hands-on approach to learning.

The vocational program includes a woodwork shop that is staffed by a highly skilled Volunteer Services Overseas worker from the United Kingdom. The youths are taught the theory of woodwork and are involved in producing woodcraft that is marketed. Mechanics, welding and plumbing are also other skills taught. The youths are also using their skills to do repair work on the compound as well as work by request from various community organizations.

Life management skills development is not only done through class sessions but forms a part of Y.E.A's core program. This year, we have had the assistance of the Belize Family Life Association (B.F.L.A.), National Organization for the Prevention of Child Abuse (N.O.P.C.A.), psychological counselor, Olive Hampton, Nurse Alicia Wade, retired teacher Mrs. Beatrice Kingston Smith, American volunteer Ms. Jeanna and the N.D.A.C.C. Various religious communities have also made Y.E.A the focus of their outreach program. After a few weeks at Y.E.A., young people begin to develop a number of very natural life management skills by virtue of the productive environment of the program.

Physical exercise and sports also form an integral part of Y.E.A's program. This teaches discipline, builds self-esteem emphasizes teamwork, and motivates the youths, as was displayed in their recent victory in the Ladyville Football Marathon.

Volunteers have contributed an invaluable service to the success of Y.E.A. over the past years. In addition to the teachers, a retired nurse, a psychologist, and several artists have given of their time. Such show of community support has had a profound impact on the attitudes of the young inmates.

A poster prominently displayed at Y.E.A. bears the motto: 'Give a man a fish; you feed him for a day. Teach him how to fish and you feed him for a lifetime.' The objective at Y.E.A. is to get the youths to take on a productive state of mind, and to function as disciplined and productive citizens even within the confines of Price Barracks. The hope is that they will learn a sense of responsibility in their approach to what confronts them in life and gain that self-control they need to deter them from a life of crime.

*Group shot of youths and staff at Youth Enhancement Academy, 1997*

# Chapter 14
# Youth for the Future Annual Report 2004

## IMPACT

The Central Statistical Office figures for 2000 show that there are 70,000 young people between the ages of 15 – 29 years old in the country of Belize. This means that young people 15 – 29 comprise 28% of the country's total population. Of these young persons between the ages of 15 – 29 years old, 40,000 or 57% of them are in school. Of the other 30,000 young persons of this age group, 7,500 or 11% of the total are unemployed and the other 22,500 or 32% are working.

This 7,500 (11%) young persons between the ages of 15 – 29 form the core target segment Youth for the Future is working with through the direct provision of job creation and enterprise development services, violence reduction and conflict resolution services, HIV/AIDS education and prevention services, and through the coordination of service-delivery in a number of other critical areas that reach them through other government departments and agencies and a number of youth-focused non-government organizations.

The other 40,000 (57%) of the young persons between the ages of 15 – 29 form the secondary target segment of Youth for the Future and they are reached directly through the provision of leadership and governance services, job creation and enterprise development services, violence reduction and conflict resolution services, productivity and volunteerism services and through collaboration with primary, secondary and tertiary level institutions throughout the country.

During the program year 2004, Youth for the Future provided youth development and empowerment services to approximately 7,080 youths both in and out of school in the following areas:

### Table 1: Youth for the Future's service provision to young persons by Outcome

| Enterprise Development | Violence Reduction | Leadership & Governance | Productivity & Volunteerism | HIV/AIDS Education /Prevention |
|---|---|---|---|---|
| Training | Training | Training | Training | Training |
| Job Placement | Job Placement | Youth Forums | Free Internet | Voluntary Counseling |
| Micro-Credit | Conflict Resolution | Youth Group Management | Community Service | Peer Education |
| PSE Preparation | Sports | Sports | | Condom Distribution |

The 7,080 young persons that accessed Youth for the Future's services in the program year 2004 account for 14.9% of the total target segment of the 47,500 youths comprised of the 40,000 youths attending primary, secondary and tertiary level educational institutions and the 7,500 unemployed, out-of-school youths.

### Graph 1: YFF's Service Provision by Outcome Expected Results

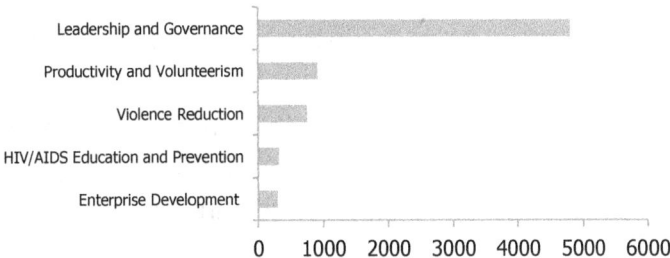

As Graph 1 above shows, the services were provided in the following amounts per Outcome expected result:

| Outcome | Number of Youths |
|---|---|
| Job Creation and Enterprise Development | 300 |
| Violence Reduction and Conflict Resolution | 750 |
| Leadership and Governance | 910 |
| Productivity and Volunteerism | 4800 |
| HIV/AIDS Education and Prevention | 320 |

## OUTCOMES

In an effort to effectively fulfill its mission of empowering young people to participate meaningfully in the present and future development of Belize at every level, Youth for the Future has six units including the Enterprise Unit headed by Mario Turton, the Violence Reduction headed by Kevin Cadle, the Governance Unit headed by Joseph Card, the National Youth Cadet Service Corp headed by Brian Mossiah and the National 4-H and Youth Development Center headed by Luke Ramos delivering five outcome expected results.

### Job Creation and Enterprise Development

The Job Creation and Enterprise Unit along with the National 4-H and Youth Development Center and the National Youth Service Cadet Corp provide job creation and enterprise development services.

The Job Creation and Enterprise Unit provide job skills and personal skills development programs focusing on increasing youth capacity for absorption into the emerging job markets. The unit also manages a youth enterprise fund that provides credit to youths for viable business ventures. It also has a job referral and information system serving as a clearinghouse for employment opportunities for young persons.

The National 4-H and Youth Development Center equips young persons 14 – 19 who are out of school with marketable skills including agriculture/vocational education, life planning and goal setting, decision-making, entrepreneurship and remedial education. The program duration is 10 months and currently has 48 students.

## Leadership and Governance

The Governance Unit is essentially the former Youth Department under a new name. This unit has offices in every district and is responsible for organizing and providing technical assistance to the urban and rural youth councils in every district, providing technical assistance to youth groups countrywide, the organizing of debates and forums discussing national issues and utilizing mock youth parliaments as a mechanism for engendering youth participation in the decision-making processes.

## Violence Reduction and Conflict Resolution

The Violence Reduction Unit and the National Youth Service Cadet Corp provide violence reduction and conflict resolution services.

The Violence Reduction Unit, in particular, provides a central base where a skilled multidisciplinary team- including police, counselors, youth workers and young people intervene to mediate and peacefully resolve potentially violent street disputes, assist young people on a self- or agency-referral basis, including via the courts and schools and provide groups of 'at risk' young people with challenging outdoor activities and group-based personal development/awareness workshops.

The National Youth Cadet Service Corp is a one-year residential program for young men between 13 – 18 years of age who are exhibiting delinquent behavior. This program is located at Mile 21 on the western Highway. The one-year program includes a booth Camp phase designed to build character through discipline, an Academic phase designed to build communication skills and a Vocational phase that introduces marketable skills training and apprenticeship. There are currently 46 Cadets in the program.

## HIV/AIDS Education and Prevention

The HIV/AIDS Education and Prevention Unit is a recent addition at Youth for the Future. Starting its service-provision in August 2004, the unit works closely with other stakeholders to train and manage peer educators, provide attitudinal and behavior change communication through training and the media to youths in especially difficult circumstances while providing voluntary counseling, referrals for testing and other services.

## Productivity and Volunteerism

The Resource and Training Center and the Governance Unit provide much YFF's productivity and volunteerism services. The Resource and Training Center, in particular, provides in-school and unattached young persons with a youth friendly environment to learn and access information through the use of 9 computers and free internet access from 8:00 a.m. –

*Insights into Gang Culture in Belize – What Worked*

8:00 p.m. daily, along with free access to reference materials and periodic IT training.

Through the accomplishment of these five outcomes expected results, Youth for the Future's six units coordinating activities nationally and collaborating with other stakeholder's implements a number of output expected results. During the program year 2004, especially, Youth for the Future underwent a series of internal restructuring that resulted in the loss of some staff members and the reassignment of others.

The end result was the enhancement of a team-oriented approach to problem solving and service delivery and the strengthening of a results-based management approach reflected in the planning, implementation and monitoring of both core and peripheral youth development and youth empowerment activities.

## OUTPUTS

### Major Accomplishments
### *Management and Administration*

- In the first quarter, senior managers received training to strengthen their capacity to use a results-based management system in the planning, implementing and monitoring of their program outputs.

- A position for Officer in Charge of Human Resources was created and filled by an existing staff member to manage personnel issues, staff capacity building and the development of an organizational culture that promotes efficiency, effectiveness and productivity.

- In accordance with the principles of cost-effectiveness, YFF introduced a number of internal controls to reduce expenditure on fuel and reduce utilities expenses at NYCSC, the Nat'l 4-H, the Governance Unit and the Secretariat. This reduced expenditure is reflected in the end-of-year records.

- A YFF Manual outlining policies governing operational procedures was developed and distributed during the program year. The manual should contribute to the maintenance of a work environment geared towards productivity and effectiveness.

- In the area of transparency and accountability, the development of a number of internal checks and balances allowed YFF to report no major loss in property or goods during the period.

- A system of monitoring consisting of regularly scheduled managers' meetings, regularly scheduled meetings at the Secretariat and regularly scheduled all-staff

*YFF staff at the end of staff retreat in Belmopan, 2003*

- Meetings, weekly task lists and weekly reports have served to improve the quality of service provided in all of YFF's units.

- In an effort to increase YFF's visibility and enhance its image among numerous stakeholders, the radio program "Opportunities Unlimited" aired on Love FM has been programmed to include coverage of the activities of other youth empowerment agencies. Similarly, a reader-friendly monthly update continues to be produced and distributed to policy-makers and other stakeholders.

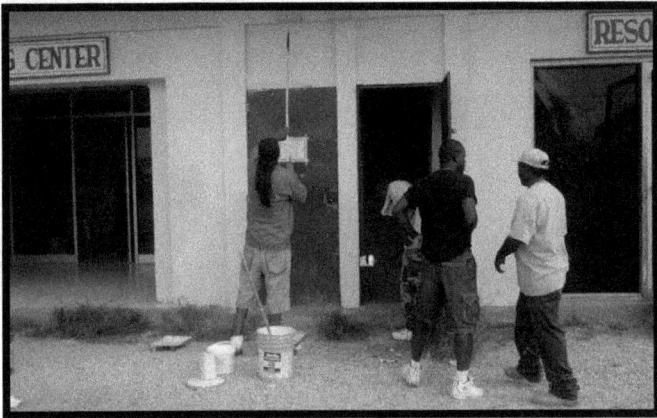

*Youths painting YFF Secretariat*

- YFF also had some success increasing its sustainability through the submission of a number of proposals. A proposal submitted to the Social Investment Fund for the construction of a dormitory at the NYCSC has been approved and the funds will be disbursed in February, 2005. Another proposal for the expansion of services in all the district centers was submitted to the Basic Needs Trust Fund and has been approved for funds disbursement in March, 2005. Two other proposals were submitted for HIV/AIDS education activities. One approved by the OPEC/UNFPA fund got underway in August 2004 and another proposal submitted to the Global Fund managed by BEST will start on March 2005. Another proposal submitted to the International Youth Foundation for

$700,000 is in the process of review for final approval expected in the 2nd or 3$^{rd}$ quarters of program year 2005.

*Job preparedness training conducted by Merlyn Young*

## *Job Creation and Enterprise Development*

- During the year, the unit saw a change of leadership from Sandra Bradshaw to Mario Turton. There also was a modification of the unit's programming where a business incubator concept was introduced to supplement existing activities such as small business development training, job placement and the provision of micro-credit. The business incubator involves YFF developing a viable business that will serve as a model business to provide practical training to young entrepreneurs. The first of these businesses has been established at the Belize Tourism Village.

- During the year, 14 loans were distributed in collaboration with the Small Farmers and Business Bank bringing the total to 62 loans amounting to close to $250,000. Although the loans disbursed amounted to a job created for a young entrepreneur, there are, nonetheless, a number of non-performing loans that required the attention of YFF personnel during the reporting period. Efforts to motivate these loan recipients into meeting their payment obligations continued during the year.

*Group photo at the end on YFF staff training session*

- In collaboration with the Violence Reduction Unit's Operation Positive Reinforcement 213 young persons were provided with jobs during the program year. The jobs were negotiated following attendance of the young persons at personal development, job preparedness and HIV/AIDS education training conducted in collaboration with BBB and UB. A significant number of these placements resulted in full-time employment for the referred youths.

- Along with the Programs Development Manager, the Enterprise Unit did research and used the data gathered to develop business plans for a youth cooperative to produce fresh orange juice targeting government schools in the first instance and all schools subsequently. In addition, the unit has been in contact with the Adult and Continuing Education section of the University of Belize to develop another cooperative to produce baked goods. The planning and implementation processes are well underway and should be implemented in the 2$^{nd}$ quarter of 2005.

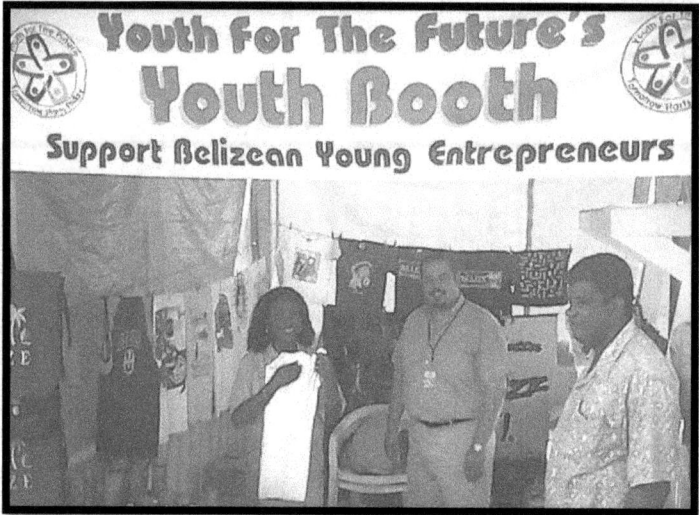

*YFF booth featuring products by young entrepreneurs. (Young entrepreneur showing off wares to Mario Thurton and Floyd "Cinco" Gladden)*

### *Leadership and Governance*

- The Governance Unit was engaged in a number of activities during the year that increased youth involvement in the decision-making processes. The highlight of the year's activities was a Youth Leaders Camp conducted at the University of Belize's Faculty of Natural Resources in Central Farm, where, out of a group of 150 youths, 110 young leaders from every district in the country completed two weeks of capacity-building sessions in a number of areas ranging from leadership to governance etc. In an effort to minimize the outlay of funds that would have been necessary for the camp, the organizers approached the private sector for assistance. The contributions they got ranged from $100 given by Black Hawk Security to

$4,000 provided by Bowen and Bowen. Below is a list of the contributors:

| | | |
|---|---|---|
| Bel Car Exports/Imports | Belize Marketing Bd. | Grace Kennedy |
| Hon. Rodwell Ferguson | University of Belize | Belize Mills Ltd. |
| Belize Family Life Assn. | Bowen and Bowen | Quality Poultry |
| Banana Growers Assn. | Running W. Meats | Crystal Water |
| Citrus Products Belize | Belize Choice Gas | Andy Palacio |
| Roses Paper Products | San Ignacio Hotel | Genesis Arts |
| Mayor David Fonseca | Ministry of Works | Scotia Bank |
| St. Anthony's Trading | GOB Press Office | Del Oro |
| Social Security Board | Hon. Mike Espat | Brodies |
| Black Hawk Security | Hon. Vildo Marin | |

- The camp also had the participation of young persons from Cuba, the United States and Mexico.

- The Governance Unit, in collaboration with a youth steering committee and its Youth Action Faction Youth Group formed with young persons attending the Youth Leaders Camp 2004 and financial assistance from private sector companies also coordinated a National Youth Week that featured activities conducted in every district. The debates, forums, marathon, etc. conducted in the districts were featured in YFF's monthly update.

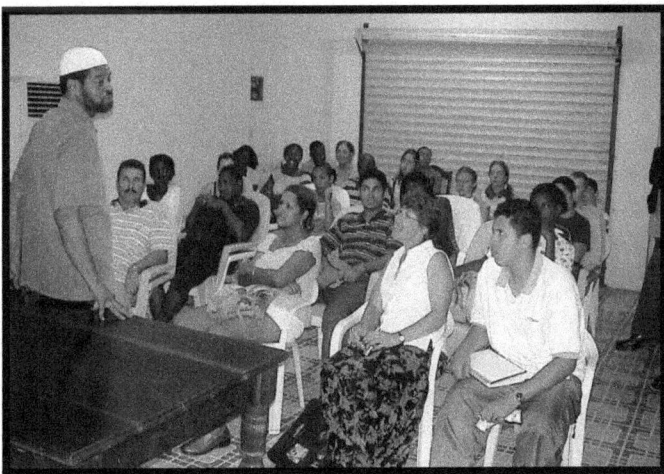

*YFF director addressing workshop*

- As a part of the Mixed Commission Agreement between Belize and Cuba, the Ministry of Education, Youth and Sports organized a one-month youth exchange program that resulted in 10 Cuban youths visiting Belize and 11 Belizean youths visiting Cuba. The exchange was the product of a visit to Cuba by Ministry of Education, Youth and Sports personnel to meet with their counterparts to expand cooperation in the areas of education, youth and sports. YFF's Executive Director, Nuri Muhammad was among the Ministry's delegates and agreed on behalf of GOB to manage and organize the exchange. The exchange resulted in the transfer of expertise in many youth empowerment areas including recruitment, activity planning and implementation, promotion etc.

*Ex-gang members at a session at the Violent Reduction Unit*

- In the 3rd quarter the Governance Unit organized a sports and culture exchange to La Isla Mujeres, Quintana Roo, Mexico in which 45 young persons representing every district attended to participate.

## *Violence Reduction and Conflict Resolution*

- In the 1st quarter of 2004, the Violence Reduction Unit of Youth for the Future in collaboration with the Belize Police Department launched Operation Positive Reinforcement. Through this one-year operation, employment, training, access to credit and counseling were provided to some of Belize's most hardcore and notorious unattached youths. Anecdotal evidence provided by the Commissioner of Police Carmen Zetina confirms that the operation had an effect in reducing the number of violent crimes that were down compared to 2003 figures.

*Sandra Bradshaw, coordinator of the Enterprise Unit with youths outside the Resource Center*

- The operation had four distinct phases: recruitment, screening and referral, training and job placement, and monitoring. During recruitment, personnel from YFF and the Police Department go into identified "hot spots" and invite individuals to access training and job placement services. During a screening and referral, profiles of the youths were developed by gathering biographical data that were stored manually and electronically. After receiving training and being placed on a job, the youths are then monitored.

Since its inception in February, the Violence Reduction Unit through OPR, recruited 750 youths in the Belize City area. Another 650 of these youths were screened and filled out forms that are currently in fill. Of this number 200 youths participated in the training activities. One hundred and seventy-five of them completed the training and received certificates and 160 of them were placed in companies including, Brodies, Princess, All Upholstery etc. S.E.L. hired 56 of them permanently as did Texaco with 2 of them, Black Hawk Security with 8 of them among others. One of three youth that was offered the opportunity of getting a loan had received funding. Another youth received training on a tour guiding at BTB. Eight other youths completed an intense two weeks H.I.V./A.I.D.S training from Red Cross of Belize, apart from YFF training, 10 was referred to the counseling center and 20 received assistance in managing existing court cases.

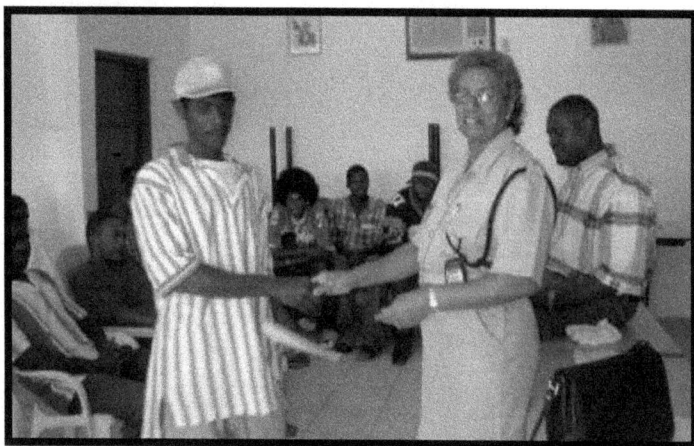

*Sr. Supt. Yolanda Murry, along with Douglas Hyde, handing out certificates at the end of Operation Positive Reinforcement program*

## *HIV/AIDS Education and Prevention*

- With HIV/AIDS reaching every corner of Belizean society it is imperative that every sector, especially the youth sector that along with the women sector is most heavily impacted by the epidemic, joined the multi-sector response. Ministry of Health records show that there have been 2,363 reported cases of HIV infections and 638 AIDS-related deaths since 1986. The adult prevalence of 2% in 2001 was the highest in the Central American region and the hardest hit sub groups are young persons between the ages of 20 – 29 years old.

- Youth for the Future has joined the fight primarily by collaborating with the National AIDS Commission and partnering with the OPC/UNFPA fund to provide peer education services to young people in especially difficult circumstances. To this effect 25 young peer educators have been trained in collaboration with PASMO, the Belize Red Cross, BFLA, HECOPAB, the National AIDS Program and AAA. They have, through personal contacts with other young people and table sessions conducted in residential locations such as the Pickstock Street "Jungle", Crawl Road, Rocky Road and other hotspots reached close to 300 other youths.

- The Minister of Education opened a "Friendly-Spaces Center" at YFF's headquarter on Youth for the Future Drive where counseling referral is provided, condoms are distributed to those who request them and training is conducted for unattached and out-of-school youth.

## *Productivity and Volunteerism*

- One of the most widely used services offered by YFF is information technology services offered through the Resource Center. On a daily basis, literally dozens of young persons including students and out-of-school youth flock to the Resource Center to complete assignments and reports and to surf the world-wide-web for information.

- The Resource Center staff has also conducted quarterly training for young persons in introduction to many of the Microsoft family of programs and the Internet. This along with personal development training conducted by Marilyn Young of the Ministry of Labor Internet facilitates youth preparation for job search.

- The Resource Center during the program year has also been responsible for the coordination of community service activities, including those that YFF coordinates in collaboration with YMCA, BYM and others that have young persons assisting elderly and underprivileged persons but those that consist of students fulfilling their community service requirements that come to YFF to provide after-school tutorials for young students in the neighborhoods among other tasks.

## CHALLENGES AND DELAYS

There are two main challenges that follow Youth for the Future into the new-year. From a macro-perspective the main challenge is developing a synergy that will last long enough to increase productivity and effectiveness. From a micro-perspective, the issue of non-performing loans in an adjusted fiscal environment may linger on and affect YFF's ability to contribute positively to the micro-credit sector and through this to the young entrepreneurs in the wider society.

- Because of the evolution of the agency, the existence of a youth department and two institutions that are geographically removed and the addition of three other elements that require implementation at this point, there is a level of fragmentation of service delivery that will require sustained attention for the first four to five years of the organization's existence.

- Senior team members accustomed to planning and implementing in isolation, do not take advantage of the synergy and economies of scale that would allow for greater efficiency, heightened effectiveness, increased productivity and the conspicuous impact that would shut up the critics and motivate the supporters to more action.

- A series of measures including the adoption of a Results Based Management System, more frequent meetings, joint unit planning, the development of transparent personnel and operational policies, training for increased capacity etc. will be undertaken over the next two years to strengthen the synergy between management staff and among other staff.

- The issue of the non-performing loans remains a critical one for Youth for the Future. Besides affecting credibility, non-performing loans reduce the availability of funds for other youth enterprises. Increased collaboration with the Small Farmers and Business Bank to track and motivate recipients to meet payment requirements will continue during 2005. In cases of non-compliance, court action will be used to force loan repayment.

## CORRECTIVE ACTIONS – 2005

Along with the maintenance of existing programs, Youth for the Future is in the process or plans to implement the following interventions:

- Enhance the legal framework of Youth For The Future through the passing of a statutory instrument governing YFF's operations.

- Enhance communication and public relations to increase YFF's visibility, and improve its image and engender popular support for the agency in communities in Belize City and the districts.

- To increase youth participation in YFF's decision-making and policy development processes.

- Strengthen the operation and management capacity of the Rural and Urban Youth Councils and the National Youth Council.

- Similar to the Education Summit, conduct a Youth Summit to provide a wide range of youth stakeholders with the opportunity to discuss critical youth issues.

- Increase productivity at district centers through the expansion of service-provision, the increase of staff and volunteer capacity and the procurement of equipment and supplies.

- Strengthen collaborative mechanisms with other youth stakeholders and consolidate a national youth agenda coordinated by Youth for the Future.

- Conduct another international youth camp widening the participation to include young people not only from the United States, Mexico and Cuba but youth from the United Kingdom, Canada, Jamaica and Guyana.

- Streamline the operations and targets of the Enterprise Unit, the Violence Reduction Unit and the HIV/AIDS Education Unit.

- Increase community participation in the community relations activities of the National Youth Cadet Service Corp.

- Increase the enterprise development focus of the National 4-H and Youth Development Center.

- Employ strategic planning processes to develop a 3-Year Plan and a synthesized one-year operational plan.

- Increase YFF's cost recovery through the production and sale of fresh orange juice to government schools in the first instance and all schools subsequently.

- Increase collaboration with IDB, the International Youth Foundation, and Tourist Industry Stakeholders to provide information technology training to young persons from every district.

# Multi Prong Approach to Dealing with Gangs

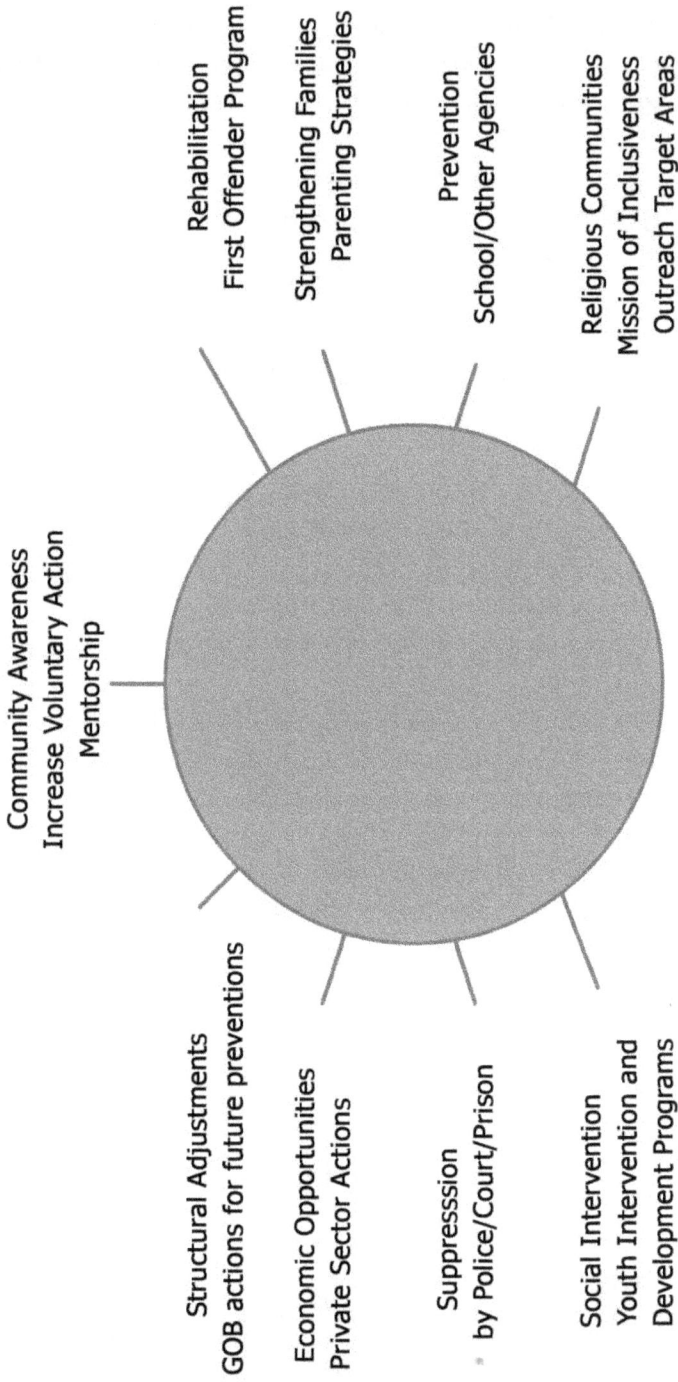

Community Awareness
Increase Voluntary Action
Mentorship

Rehabilitation
First Offender Program

Strengthening Families
Parenting Strategies

Prevention
School/Other Agencies

Religious Communities
Mission of Inclusiveness
Outreach Target Areas

Structural Adjustments
GOB actions for future preventions

Economic Opportunities
Private Sector Actions

Suppresssion
by Police/Court/Prison

Social Intervention
Youth Intervention and
Development Programs

# Chapter 15
# Yabra Community Policing Project

Belize City police continue to face an increase in the number of calls from the public. This is especially so on the Southside of the city where statistically the majority of crimes occur. There is also a growing recognition by the police that traditional methods of addressing the fight against crime and disorder cannot be sustained without the involvement through partnership of citizens from those communities where crime occurs. Unless new and innovative methods are used to encourage members of the community to partner with the police through various programs designed to combat crime and make Belize City safer we will remain in a reactionary mode that will be increasingly more costly in terms of public safety, police human resource and public expenditure.

The establishment of a Community Policing Unit Center (C.P.U.C.) in the 'Yabra' area of Belize City is an attempt to proactively address the frequency of crime in this area by developing programs based on the partnership between the police and the community. The foundation of a successful community policing strategy is the close mutually beneficial ties between the police and community members. As this proposal will outline, the benefits of establishing this Center are not only realizable, but considering the tremendous savings in lives, property, and public expenditure, it is an absolute necessity in making Belize City safer.

## RATIONALE

The rationale for establishing a C.P.U.C. in the 'Yabra' area of Belize City is grounded in the need to employ new and innovative methods in tackling the problems of crime, violence, delinquency and neighborhood decay in this area. The Police Department has primarily focused on reactive crime fighting strategies in these areas. These measures have not brought the measure of relief to the situations as expected and therefore it has become incumbent on the Department to adopt new and innovative approaches to policing while the fundamental objective – a safer Belize -- remains the same.

The C.P.U.C. therefore promises much for building and improving relations with the Belize City public in general, and to effectively deal with crime and activities leading to crime and blight in the 'Yabra' area specifically. It is a deliberate attempt to nurture existing good relations and open more avenues for individuals and groups to articulate their problems to the police who are willing to listen. Mothers with children affected by violence, youth wanting to break free of the cycle of crime/violence, victims of domestic violence, street children, the destitute and underprivileged will all become an important concern to the police as are criminals. It is clearly established that these cases and their social circumstances all give rise to crime. Therefore, between the police and the community working together to relieve the effect of these social scourges is a critical approach to crime management and prevention.

This initiative therefore must go beyond only the community policing unit and the 'Yabra' community and must also include other Government and N.G.O. agencies, the business community and other civic organizations to generate the resources needed to get the job done.

## OBJECTIVES

The objectives of the C.P.U.C are:

- To promote better understanding of the police's role in the community

- To develop closer working relationships with the community and keep open lines of communication between citizens and the Police Department

- To give leadership and support to activities in the community that will lead to human betterment and progress.

- To help develop and maintain relationships between the police and community groups, organizations and schools.

- To collaborate with members of the community in developing police sponsored programs to help reduce crimes.

- To work with educational institutions to improve relations with youth in the community.

- To help communities resolve their problems – especially youth in conflict

- To assist in maintaining a positive public image of the Belize Police Department

## OPERATIONAL OVERVIEW

The Yabra Citizens Development Committee (Y.C.D.C.) is a model of community and police working together for a safer

Belize. The initiative started as a group of grieving mothers who had lost a child to violence. After several meetings the group eventually started to focus on the root causes for their grief: crime and violence and the decay that it brought to the community. This group of mothers realized that their community had become the victim of senseless violence and was being held hostage to crime. They decided to do something to take back their community. They first expanded their membership to include men and youths. Then the first task of the group was mobilization to inform the rest of the community of their purpose and objectives.

The group members canvassed the community. They also held meetings where issues of concern to the community were discussed. These meetings are held regularly and have become an important forum for discussing community/police relations. Critical and sensitive matters have been brought up at these meetings where emotions sometimes run high, because the community over the years has experienced a negative relationship with the police. Channels of communication were non-existent and the situation could be described as one of 'us' and 'them.' Police were seen as a "force" that came in to the community to do a job (investigate and arrest) then left and not seen as being a part of the community, despite the fact that so many police officers live in the said community.

From these public meetings have come ideas of how the community views police activities in the community. Where criticisms were warranted they were given in an open and respectable manner. These interchanges also gave the police a forum for engaging the residents to work together in activities that would improve the overall safety in the community. Because the police involvement in this group has been a supportive one in the background and not as part of any executive position, the partnership has been a dynamic one. The police have supported activities of Y.C.D.C. by providing logistical support to its initiative. The systematic relationship has shown the police to be a supporter of youths to improve conditions in the community instead of the landlord role of being an "outside force."

At present the Yabra area has the highest murder rate in the country and one of two trouble spots where gang rivalry wants to rear its ugly head once again. It is critical that we establish a police presence in this area, not just the police in their traditional format, but as a C.P.U.C., which puts an emphasis on working with the community in addressing those issues that lead to crime and lack of safety in the community.

## DROP-IN CENTER

The C.P.U.C. will also operate as a Drop-In Center where the residents of the community can drop in at any time of the day. It is proposed that an on-site technical person will be available on a daily basis to answer questions where possible and make referrals, where necessary, to assist residents.

It is proposed that space at the Center be available to our partners in human and community services to provide their services to this area of the city. Services provided by the Women's Department, Community Rehabilitation, Y.F.F., N.D.A.C.C., Young Women's Christian Association, Young Men's Christian Association, A.I.D.S. Commission and others can all be accommodated. Due to the stigma and discrimination that has affected this area, the availability of services have been limited, sometimes due to security concerns. The presence of a C.P.U.C. in this community will change that. The Center will provide a 24/7 police presence in the community and therefore provide a safe haven from which many other service providers can operate.

## COMMUNITY BASED PROGRAMS

Additionally, the Center will facilitate the following services to the community and provide a coordinating office for community based initiatives like the Y.C.D.C.

- *After-school Internet Café:* Provide students Internet access to assist with school assignments. Provide Information technology training to bridge the digital divide and make community residents computer literate.

- *Counseling Center:* Provide community with access to counseling services.

- *Quick Response to Conflict:* Be ready to intervene in early stages of conflict among community residents, especially youth. Provide training in peaceful resolution of conflicts.

- *Training Outlet:* The Center will provide space for short-term community empowerment training in a wide variety of areas to increase the capacity of community residents to tackle the issues facing the community. Training will include, but not limited to, leadership, advocacy, budgeting, managing small business, etc.

The establishment of a C.P.U.C. to serve as a coordinating center for the Community Policing Program as well as providing an operational center for other service to the community by service providers, including government, private sector and N.G.Os is a model for the future.

*Insights into Gang Culture in Belize – What Worked*

Community Policing initiatives have been limited to partnership between the police and the community; however, this initiative broadens the partnership to include other agencies and groups which sometimes reduce their service to marginalized sectors of the community, because of safety and security concerns. This initiative has succeeded in providing a safe haven for other service providers to execute programs much needed by the community.

We will not change the crime statistics without a change in our own way of thinking and the way we do things. Many of us do not want to admit that we have become a part of the status quo and this is the problem. We lament the past days when things were more innocent and we loved each other more. Well, those days are gone, with new circumstances replacing them; but what is not gone is the power of love and good relationships especially when it comes from the family. We are on the right tract when we encourage mentorship programs for boys and girls to help them through their rites of passage from youth to adulthood. We are on the right track when we form community groups to increase security in our neighborhoods and schools. We are on track when we use our voice to advocate for those things that we know are right. We are on track when we see beyond the confines of our narrow political party construct to see the love for Belize as our uncompromising passion.

# Section III
# The Way Forward

## Chapter 16
## Boys to Men

When Mrs. Sandra Cadle, Counsellor at Edward P. Yorke High School, first asked me to write an article about the process of boys to men that young black males go through in Belize, I was hesitant. I thought that many had gotten sick and tired of hearing about the woes of black boys and would be turned off; one more article would only be skimmed through and cynically dismissed with the retort: "nuff said". But she was persistent and felt that there was need for more debate on this issue and therefore convinced me that there is still much more that needs to be said.

Much has been said about the marginalization of young black males in Belize and the statistics of the criminal justice system, the educational system and the labor force survey, all indicate that this sector of the population has been in a state of crisis for the last two decades. There is no question that we are dealing with a crisis situation that requires sustained actions directed at this sector if we are to make a real difference. By now I am sure we realize that what we are seeing played out on our nightly news and weekend papers is a reflection of a potentially explosive situation in our social order and not just random acts of crime and violence.

We should by now realize that this is not "one or two rude boy who just need a lashing"; rather this is a culture that is growing with increasing self-justification. This is not something that will go away with "stiff police action to root out criminals." It is a much more ingrained social behavior that will not go away with external action aimed only at punishment without a genuine effort to make structural changes in our socio-economic order and tackle head on the issue of distributive justice which remains the underlying challenge when dealing with the broader issue of youth and crime. We must engage these youth in proactive ways of addressing this problem of crime taking into consideration these factors.

When the Human Development Ministry or the National Committee for Families and Children (NCFC) say that they are focused on the problems of children, what do they mean? While the UN definition of children is anyone under 18 years old that sector of boys who are 15, 16, 17 years old and involved in crime and violence are not considered in that discourse. The assumption is that what we are seeing with youth violence is a manifestation of individual pathology of boys coming from dysfunctional families, rather than a systemic widespread problem affecting a significantly large sector of our male youth population. Therefore, while the Ministry, and by extension the NCFC, supposedly look for solutions to address those issues affecting "our children", this other sector of our children are left to the criminal justice system to address.

There is still the naive assumption that all these boys need is some 'tough love' and that will resolve the problem, but the stark cold reality is that young black males, in Belize City especially, have become an endangered species. When you realize what is going on you must conclude that more urgent than the monkey, the manatee, the jaguar, protected areas that these youth require an immediate, appropriate and comprehensive response.

The statistics tell us that over the last ten years homicide has been one of the major causes of death of Belizeans, and this sector of the population has the highest number of those murdered. Clearly a trend or pattern can be observed that young black males are more likely to die by violence. If we take other statistics like health such as H.I.V. and other S.T.Is, we again see alarming figures.

The atmosphere of hostility and conflict that many young black males go through in the city decrease their chances of living a normal life. Violence and its impact on the human population is a major health concern of the World Health Organization, (WHO): " It is critical that we examine those trends and take the appropriate responses to combating them." Our response must be multi-faceted since we are not dealing with a contained problem. The issue of young males dealing with the current atmosphere of hostility is really deeper than just the prospects for violence they meet; it is more their learning how to make choices and be responsible for their behavior, and at its root this requires providing these youths a knowledge of themselves and models through mentorship to assist them through their rites of passage.

These youths are victims of type casting or profiling. A black male youth is likely to get the attention of the security personnel at the grocery or department store. His being stopped by police for routine searches is such a common occurrence now that it no longer raises the eyebrow of the passerby who assumes, because of typecasting, that they must be guilty of something. In school there is also an assumption that they are lazy and low achievers; it is assumed that they will be in the largest percentile of below average students; it is assumed that they will be the most distracted with extra-curricular activities; it is assumed that they will be the smallest number going on to tertiary level education.

In family life and relationships, again there is a stereotyping that generates the assumptions about young black males. It is assumed that they are the most irresponsible in relationships and are least faithful to their mate. It is assumed that they are too selfish and self-centered to enjoy lasting relationships, and that they abandon their children more often than any other group. That most of them are from single mothers' homes where their fathers had abandoned them, and that most of them have substance abuse problems and come from families with substance abuse problems, and that they are more violent to their women and children than other groups.

These assumptions also apply to the workplace and therefore it is assumed that the young black male is lazy and wants something for nothing. It is assumed that he will do the smallest amount of work and demand the highest pay. It is assumed that he is not ambitious nor has a vision of anything beyond a payday. That he is more interested in party and sport, than ambitions for the future. It is assumed that he will never control any enterprise of substance because this culture of laziness is so deeply rooted in him.

None of this is true because it's all generalization of a problem that has deeper implication than the superficial overstatement that is normally used to describe it, but despite this, it still has an influence on how these black youths are viewed by many Belizeans.

I think to a great extent we have only marginally focused on these problems and its various causes over the last twenty-five years. Dr. Jawanza Kunjufu, educational consultant and author and president of African American Images in Chicago, has articulated that there are four phases to problem solving. First there is the identification of the problem itself. Then there is the understanding of the roots and the causes of the problem. After which comes a plan of action for dealing with the problem; and finally the implementation of that plan.

On the issue of young black males in Belize we have spent marginal time on all four phases. We have marginally defined the problem, not being specific in identifying areas where the problem was worse. In trying to understand the roots of the problem we were not scientific in our approach which left our conclusion to be filled with assumptions, conjectures and innuendos not founded on any research or analysis of what were the real day to day maladies that face this sector, and what really causes them to act the way they do.

As far as plans of action were concerned we have made many attempts in addressing this problem, however, the problem with most of those plans of action was the impromptu or spontaneous manner in which they came about. In most instances they were responses to opportunities provided by circumstances to work with this sector. The C.Y.D.P. experiment was one such example of that. It was not a planned program but one that came as a response provided by the historical truce of February 1995. In a way this program sought to respond programmatically to issues that very little research had gone into beforehand to direct the program to specific needs to service this sector. So these programs provide a 'net-catch-all' approach rather than being specifically focused on needs based on previously accessed problem/analysis through research.

Finally, the implementation was usually beneficial to the youths in the short term but not sustainable over any long period that made the purpose for the initiative a "fraud" in the eyes of many of youth. Why excite these youths with the idea that real change will be made in their lives when in reality none of these programs that offer them temporary relief from their everyday struggle will be sustained beyond a few months?

But when it comes right down to Belize in 2006, what can we say to these youths? Most people today are not concerned about what these youths may have gone through or are going through in their life. Today, Belize is not concerned about your past; it is concerned about what you bring to the table by way of knowledge and skills. Many black youths today want to rely on the "look what they did to me" or the victim argument, but find that there is no sympathy for those who are not actively trying to make a difference in their lives. Belize today is filled with people in disadvantageous positions. Central Americans who number in the tens of thousands, Africans, Asians, Americans, Europeans, and Caribbean, all in Belize looking for an opportunity to progress. So there is no sympathy for the black youth who relies on the "sympathy card", in a time when you must prove yourself.

If we start to look at the process from boys to men we must start with where our boys are today. Sometimes when we entertain these ideas we get carried away with the dream concept of a boy through his effort growing up to be a great man, when in reality, if he is minimally successful in his effort, he will just be an ordinary man, with no frills or fanfare, and that is the crux of the matter. The real rites of passage is a natural organic process that takes place every second of that young male's life, whether there is a structured program to direct it or it finds its own self direction.

The idea of a 'Rites of Passage' has become a buzz term to describe the process that a young man grows into their manhood. African tribal tradition has been used to drive home the point that there needs to be a ritual process to bring boys into their manhood as was done in the past. This ceremony has gained popularity in many African American communities that institute rites of passage ceremonies for their young. But while there is much ceremony given to these rituals the process of a boy to a man is organic, real and dynamic whether there is an established ritual or not. A boy will imitate his way to manhood if he has no model to emulate.

The process from boyhood to manhood is a challenging one and there is no model or one size that fits all so the trial and error process is one fraught with frustration for young Belizean males. Growing up is not the same for all young men, the multiplicity of situations that now exist socially, economically, morally, etc, is far different than fifty years ago. Those were tough days, but there was a moral discipline that under-pinned our social behavior and our role as men was clear, but today that code is being challenged from so many directions and that code is no longer accepted as the only 'code of conduct' by which social behavior is judged. Today you can get away with almost any kind of behavior particularly if is immoral but not illegal. A young man today has a wide margin of error in evaluating his behavior even to the point where anything goes. Naturally many get lost on this road. This blurred moral relativity defies criticism since its every man for himself, 'so mind your business'. There is no social moral standard that serves as the single criterion for judging the right from the wrong approach.

Even the standard set by religion has been blurred and veils the revolutionary power of religion. Religion has been watered down to 'Churchianity' and has lost its appeal to the majority of young men who are seeking strong moral leadership and not just religion. While many youths in their early years are involved with the church the trend seems to be that most lose that strong connection in their late teens and by their twenties they are only marginally attached to organized religious ceremonies. Most continue their strong belief in a supreme being and acknowledge the universal law of right over wrong and truth over falsehood but they are not contained by any religious doctrine nor attend any established religious sanctuary. The exception to this is the rise in young men attracted to Islam and the Rastafarian movement. Both communities have a unique appeal to the young black male searching for an identity of manhood in the midst of a moral relative society and therefore have a disproportionate number of young black males in their membership. Why is this?

So I have to agree with Mrs. Cadle that there is yet much to be discussed in this issue of our young black males reaching their rightful places as productive men in our society. The challenges facing this sector are complex and cannot be approached without taking into consideration all factors.

# Chapter 17
# Cyclical Pattern of Crime

There has been a cyclical pattern of crime in Belize that goes back over 25 years. In 1987 we were looking at the beginnings of gang activity in Belize. This was a first for Belize which before had only seen youths, ('base boys'), hanging out at the bases. That was a time when the most serious crimes confronting the Police, were petty theft, burglary, possession of weed and the occasional murder. That climate began to change drastically in the late eighties with the influence of the international drug and arms trade which spilled over into Belize and transformed our country in more ways than one; most notably that section of society we called street youths.

The international drug trade has changed the climate of crime in the whole Caribbean and this tidal wave of drugs, money, guns, violence and its corrupting influence in high places, has changed the region forever. Issues ranging from money laundering to common street crimes, and the proliferation of the so-called gang warfare between rival groups, are all the influence of this movement of drugs through our region heading for the North American market.

This alluring trade brought quick cash to an underclass of unskilled, untrained, and high risked youths, who became tools in a trade that requires violence to control one's turf. Many of our youths have died uselessly in this ongoing war of fratricide, (brother killing brother).

The road ahead requires a multi-pronged approach to dealing with youths, crime and violence, and a major aspect of that approach must continue to be the national security perspective. Clearly these youths are only pawns in a sophisticated organized criminal network and are in no way real players in the criminal equation; however, by their criminal activities they have created a disequilibrium affecting the social order that threatens citizen security. It is therefore essential to break this sophisticated, organized crime network from the practice of using these youths to facilitate their drug trade. Therefore decisive interdiction operations must continue to disrupt this network and to detain all those found to be a part of the operation of distributing drugs in and though Belize especially those in high places.

What we face today is more problematic than the gang activities of a decade or more ago. Today's crime is defined by increased random acts of violence by youths, primarily male against male, who have no defined gang affiliation. These acts of violence are motivated by an increased attitude of bravado and hostility among our youth and the availability of guns and the fast dollar made from drugs. While these youths may individually express gang affiliations their criminal patterns are not consistent with what international research say about gang war between rival gangs.

There is therefore a cadre of youths whose propensity for violence has increased to alarming proportions. The climate of anarchy against established authority at all levels creates the prototype of a criminal that can best be described as a 'sociopath', i.e., a person having no understanding or concern about established social order. This type of youth is not easy to "rehabilitate", since they were never given a basic framework of civility in their upbringing. Many are the children of children. This is a dilemma for those involved in the rehabilitation process; the question is: how can a youth be rehabilitated (returned) when he has nothing structured to return to in the first place?

The fact is we are seeing a cyclical drama being played out; the same core problems remain and the current murder statistics are only symptoms of a deeper set of problems. But we continue to pass this way, each time missing the opportunity to use the crisis as a catalyst to tackle these problems once and for all. Clearly we have numerous reports, dating as far back as the Crime Commissions of 1992 and 2000, to verify that the core problems remain the same. We know what those problems are and we also know what works in dealing with them. We have had several models of successful interventions by both the government and N.G.Os in addressing this problem.

The greater challenge in approaching this problem, however, will require greater vision and a deeper financial commitment to pay for it. As said before, we know what is required to address this problem. We have seen what works, but are we committed to bringing about real change? Do we have the political will? Unfortunately we as a country have not been decisive about this problem; chartering a twenty year plan of action for the social, economic and spiritual transformation of these youth. While there have been many attempts or programs including C.Y.D.P., Y.E.A., the Cadet Corps and Y.F.F., they have remained short term projects and not provided the resource to make them sustainable for the long haul.

Remember that what we see being played out in the nightly news is a repeat of what we have been seeing and hearing over the last twenty-five years and is a clear indication that we are locked in a cyclical crime pattern in Belize. We can only break that cycle when we become long-range in our vision of what measures we will put in place to mitigate the re-occurrence of the scourge of crime.

# Chapter 18
## Need for A National Crime Plan

We are seeing a rising tide of youth homicide throughout the Caribbean. Each year the number of deaths escalates. It seems as if the present plans that regional governments have set in place are not working and the murder rate continues to rise in all our territories. The 'carrot and stick' policy is a recurring strategy used by governments because of the demand by the public to appear tough on crime on the one hand, while at the same time trying to entice youth to change their criminal ways. The facts show that these strategies have had very little effect in recent years on the rate of homicide.

Although we continue to take an alarmist approach to this issue, the fact is that the solution to the problem of crime is not all that complex. If we focus for example, on the youth involvement in crime, the matter is quite simple; after all, it is known that where youths are gainfully employed, incidences of crime go down. It is also known that there is a direct relationship between a young person having access to employment or educational opportunities and the recurrence of crime. So why are we approaching the problem as if it is new and requires 'rocket science'? We know the solutions; we know what works. Now we have to get the funding to implement and the political will to sustain those solutions for the long haul.

We know that the two most important priorities are opportunities for employment and education/training. Once we ensure that those who want to work or attend some kind of school can do so, we will reduce the criminal element down to a measurable group of misfits that any Police Department can handle. However, unless the opportunity for work/school is provided, we will continue to mix up the wheat and tares. It's not until the harvest of opportunities is manifested that we will be able to discern those youths who are industrious from those who are seemingly lazy. Our young people need to have their goals, values and priorities in order, but do they even know the importance of having a goal?

If 'youth, crime and violence' was seen as a 'national security' issue the expenditure would be there. But at this time government defines 'national security' only in military terms and therefore allocates all of its 'national security' budget to military implements; however, if government was serious about combating this low-intensity warfare that is growing gradually in Belize City they would commit a significant part of their 'national security' budget to combat the problem in a broad based manner.

A fifty million dollar commitment, (in the form of grant-aid, technical assistance, equipment, tools, etc.) could begin to stem the tide of youth crime at the street level. A government serious about youth development would find creative ways of accessing funds and other forms of assistance from sources, including but not limited to the Caribbean Development Bank (C.D.B.), the Inter-American Development Bank (I.D.B.), the European Union (E.U.), Taiwan, the Organization of the Petroleum Exporting Countries (O.P.E.C.) Fund, and the Kuwaiti Fund. Government has access to some of the best proposal writers. All these entities could entrain a comprehensive national plan of action to revitalize and rejuvenate youth to become productive citizens. Their support, of course, would be contingent on the built-in sustainability of any such plan. If government can find bilateral partnerships to enhance and strengthen our infrastructure, tourism and economic sector, why can't we do the same for our human sector?

As stated above, employment generation must be a priority. Providing employment for high risked youth will pay huge dividends when the statistics of crime begin to fall. Time and time again, researchers have proven that there is a direct correlation between crime and poverty. Investment in employment opportunities will reduce crime. What greater way is there to quantify those dividends than to see a reduction in the present high cost of crime.

# Chapter 19
# Turning Prison into a Training Camp

Once again we have reached a crisis point with our youths in Belize City; this is not the first nor will it be the last if we continue to do the same thing every time we reach this critical point. It is said that only crazy people do the same thing over and over expecting different results. We have been down this road before; do we expect something different to happen this time? I do not doubt the sincerity of anyone involved in this process; I think that we all genuinely want to see change, even if it's only to see the senseless killing come to an end. But it takes more than sincerity to stop the plague of crime that has become endemic in our urban culture. This is a systemic problem and it will take a systematic solution.

It has been proven through scientific research that where jobs and educational opportunities exist the crime rate goes down. The majority of our youths are good people and they only turn bad because of anger, frustration and a rage that comes when they think that they are being left out of opportunities they see others enjoying and think they deserve. If we take a systematic approach to analyzing the problem we see that one of the breeding grounds for criminals is the prison at Hattieville; it is a 'university of crime.' But how are we dealing with the continued overflow at the prison? For every ten that leaves the prison, seven returns. This is alarming.

We are currently housing close to 1,500 inmates in our prison at an annual budget of about seven million dollars from the government of Belize. That is an average of nearly five thousand dollars per inmate annually. Added to this is the annual budget allocations for the police and the Judiciary, which includes the Magistracy, most of which goes into processing these youths through the criminal justice system. When we add to this already high figure the cost of health, education and other human services to youths revolving through the criminal justice system we get an idea of the astronomical waste of valuable resources on a sector who, in their most productive years of 14 – 25, is costing tax payers volumes to keep them in their unproductive state, many of them as repeat offenders.

According to prison officials the majority of that yearly $5,000 per inmate goes into maintenance such as feeding, sheltering and bare minimal services, including salaries for prison staff. In other words, we are warehousing bodies instead of instituting a systematic rehabilitation program with an aim of getting value for dollar out of the money expended each year. Clearly turning the prison into a training center, for the majority of inmates who are not violent felons, is an opportunity waiting to happen. The amount of idle time presently spent by inmates at the prison is scandalous; many have absolutely nothing to do all day but waste time. These people can learn a trade as they produce much needed agricultural, furniture, poultry, meats, etc. for hospitals, schools, and the poor.

A variety of vocational skills can be provided within the facility. There should be no less than 400 inmates per day involved in some form of vocational training, i.e. construction skills, furniture making and repair, plumbing, electrical, mechanic, tailoring, etc. Agricultural activities should serve as a training opportunity for inmates that will lead to some form of production, i.e. eggs or vegetables or other things that can be marketed and the proceeds go to reduce the cost of administration of these programs.

Classes where inmates are actually sitting at a desk in a classroom situation doing the kind of structured work by teachers in a structured and disciplined way towards passing very specific exams. Training in literacy, in numeracy, and communication skills development done by retired teachers will better prepare these inmates for the work force when they leave the prison. Rehabilitation should not be confined to just preaching sermons and giving lectures in self-help addiction programs but also in teaching personal responsibility and giving inmates a chance to pay their "debt' to society by working hard for 8 – 10 hours a day in productive activities that will reduce the overall cost of housing them during their prison sentence.

The average inmate today leaves the prison the same way they entered, sometimes worse because there is no serious investment in a rehabilitation process. For those who are hardcore there should be a special camp away from Hattieville, deep in the jungle by Salamanca where access to cell phones and visits by relatives is seriously restricted during their time of incarceration. At this camp there should also be a training which includes providing foods and raising animals for their own consumption. Such a challenging environment would be a deterrent to crime and would discourage youths from wanting to return to prison.

We must change this unproductive reactionary method of dealing with our crime situation and become proactive in approaching the problem in a systematic way. We have to turn around this waste of scarce resources into the bottomless pit of the present prison situation and revisit the concept of rehabilitation as a strategy of investment for increasing the productivity of these incarcerated youth rather than warehousing them as we are presently doing. To do that, in fact, requires a scientific approach to this aspect of rehabilitation. What is needed is a rehabilitation plan of action to be instituted within the prison that will incorporate and streamline all the existing programs and add to them additional programs and opportunities that will come from cooperation with agencies within government and N.G.Os and community based groups. This cooperative network will provide the opportunity for expanded programs available under the umbrella of rehabilitation.

Generally the concept of rehabilitation is applied to any activity that attempts to reform the inmate and challenge him to change his lifestyle while in the institution by providing him with access to programs and opportunities for him to grow in skills, to build capacity, to prepare him to make a change from his criminal lifestyle to the life of a productive citizen. In general terms, any activity within a prison, whether it is religious, educational or any form of training is considered activity of rehabilitation. However, while these programs are an important factor within any institution, if they are not structured their impact is lessened and is less capable of being quantified; therefore their 'value for dollar' cannot be measured.

What is presently missing in the Belize prison system is a structured rehabilitation program that takes the inmate through a process that starts from his entrance into the institution; one that can be monitored, measured and evaluated for its human as well as financial impact. To start with, not everybody can be rehabilitated, and therefore there must be a willingness on the part of the individual inmate to take advantage of the opportunity within the prison system to change his life. There should be a merit and demerit system that is based on what I call the 'snake and ladder' concept; that each inmate is aware that while he will have opportunities within the institution to climb the ladder, he

*Insights into Gang Culture in Belize – The Way Forward*

must also be aware that if he put his head in the snake's mouth by violating the rules of the institution he will end up losing those opportunities. This culture must be established within the institution.

These innovative activities should create a different atmosphere within the prison because a missing element within the prison today is hope. A structured rehabilitation program will provide that sense of hope for inmates that genuinely want the opportunity to change their lives. For those who want to stay in their cell and rot, the choice is theirs. This initiative should not be looked upon as any attempt to go soft on criminals. It will be a stern, corrective and structured program of rehabilitative activities that will be monitored on a daily basis to ensure that goals are being met. This structured approach will offer opportunities for inmates to gain structure and discipline in their lives, to build their character around some form of ethic and values, so that in that sustained environment they can perhaps get a grip on their lives and return to society as a better informed person than when they went in.

More important, it will reduce the high cost of the criminal justice system which now exceeds well over 100 million dollars annually, and which continues to drain this economy with no measurable value for dollar, nor any end in sight.

# Chapter 20
# From Truce to Peace

The current "Truce", which appears to be rapidly disintegrating is an attempt to recapture an opportunity similar to what existed in February of 1995 when all the 14 active gangs in Belize City came together to put an end to violence and death caused by gang rivalry. That historical event took place on February 18, 1995, when a peace declaration called the "Bird's Isle Declaration", was signed by all gang representatives and also signed by the then Minister of National Security and Deputy Prime Minister, Dean Barrow.

But there are some fundamental elements missing from this latest effort, most important is that a truce cannot work without the youth gang members themselves owning it and having direct input in the process of its direction. After all, it is they who have to sustain the truce. There should have been some kind of council or representative body of the gang leaders themselves with one of them becoming the "voice and the face of the truce". Instead this is a government led truce with only Ministers speaking for the status of the truce while the gang members remain props.

The first truce had youth leaders who told their own story to the community through the media. They formed themselves into a community-based organization, (CBO), made up of members from previously rival gangs. While there were ongoing rivalries, they put those conflicts on hold and supported the truce, which police records showed lasted for a year with only minor violations. These youth leaders saw the "truce" as a step toward a bigger goal of a "sustained peace" and the cessation of all conflict. They were also involved in giving back to the community through a "restitution" type service. In other words, there were "conscious youth" that made up the first C.Y.D.P. Today however, while youths are the main protagonists in the drama of street crimes they remain marginal to the decision-making process of the truce and not represented in any significant way when it comes to direction.

It would be useful to look back at this pattern of criminality to draw some lessons for the way forward. Firstly, there has been a cyclical pattern of crime in Belize that goes back over 25 years. In 1987 we were looking at the beginnings of gang activity in Belize. This was a first for Belize which before had only seen youths, ('base boys'), hanging out at the bases. That was a time when the most serious crimes confronting the police, were petty theft, burglary, possession of weed and the occasional murder. That climate began to change drastically in the late 1980s with the influence of the international drug and arms trade which spilled over into Belize and transformed our country in more ways than one; most notably that section of society we called street youths, or gangs.

The international cocaine trade has changed the climate of crime in the whole Caribbean and this tidal wave of drugs, money, guns, violence and its corrupting influence in high places, has changed the region forever. Issues ranging from money laundering to common street crimes, and the proliferation of the so-called gang warfare between rival groups, are all the influence of this movement of cocaine through our region heading for the North American market. This alluring trade brought quick cash to an underclass of unskilled, untrained, and high risked youths, who became tools in a trade that requires violence to control one's turf. Many of our youths have died uselessly in this ongoing war of fratricide, (brother killing brother).

The road ahead requires a multi-pronged approach in dealing with youths, crime and violence, and a major aspect of that approach must continue to be the national security perspective. Clearly these youths are only pawns in a more sophisticated organized criminal network and are in no way real players in the criminal equation, however, by their criminal activities, they have created disequilibrium in the social order that threatens citizen security and therefore gets the most police attention. It is therefore essential to break this sophisticated, organized crime network from the practice of using these youths to facilitate their drug trade. Therefore decisive interdiction operations must continue to disrupt this network and to detain all those found to be a part of the operation of using our youths to distribute drugs in and though Belize.

What we face today is more problematic than the gang activities of a decade and a half ago. Today's crime is defined by increased random acts of violence by youths, primarily male against male, who have no defined gang affiliation. These acts of violence are motivated by an increase attitude of bravado and hostility among our youth and the availability of high caliber guns and the fast dollar made from some hustle, whether drugs or otherwise. While these youths may individually express gang affiliations their criminal patterns are not consistent with gang war between rival gangs.

Today we are faced with a cadre of youths whose propensity for violence and savagery has increased to alarming proportions. The climate of anarchy against established authority at all levels, creates the prototype of a criminal that can best be described as a 'sociopath', i.e., a person having no understanding or concern about established social order. These youths are not easy to "rehabilitate", since they were never given a basic framework of civility in their upbringing. Many are the children of children. This is a dilemma for those involved in the rehabilitation process; the question is: how can you rehabilitate (return) a youth when he has nothing structured to return to in the first place?

The fact is we are seeing a cyclical drama being played out; the same core problems remain and the current murder statistics are only symptoms of a deeper set of problems. But we continue to pass this way, each time missing the opportunity to use the crisis as a catalyst to tackle these problems once and for all. Clearly we have numerous reports, dating as far back as the Crime Commissions of 1990 and 2000, to verify that the core problems remain the same. We have the 2010 report (Male Social Participation and Violence Research for the Belize Project) by Dr. Herbert Gayle(9), Anthologist of Social Violence of the University of the West Indies that verifies the same underlying causes. We know what those problems are and we also know what works in dealing with them. We have had several best practice models of successful interventions over the years by both the government and N.G.Os in addressing this problem.

The greater challenge in approaching this problem however, will require greater vision and a deeper financial commitment to pay for it. As said before, we know what is required to address this problem we have seen what works, but are we committed to bringing about real change? Do we have the political will? Unfortunately we as a country have not been decisive about this problem; charting a twenty-year plan of action for the social, economic and spiritual transformation of these youth was never a part of the agenda. While there have been many attempts or programs including C.Y.D.P., Y.E.A., Cadet Corps, Y.F.F. and now, Restore Belize, they have remained short term, knee-jerk projects, and not provided the resource to make them sustainable. Additionally, the most important element missing from today's effort is the absence of youth leaders leading the effort. We must put responsibility for this process of change back in the hands of the affected youths. They must own the process and they must be the ones to move the process from truce to peace.

# Section IV
# Stray Thoughts

## Chapter 21
## Knock It Off

Many young black males today can be described as being affected by a kind of "chip on the shoulder" syndrome. What is this syndrome? According to the dictionary a 'syndrome' is a matrix of behavior 'characterized by deeply held customs and mores which causes those affected to act in certain ways'. Imagine being deprived of opportunities regardless of how hard you tried or how qualified you were. Gradually, anger overtakes you, and you become cynical, condemning everybody else's attempt. This syndrome causes those affected to become paranoid, negative, and disruptive in their behavior. It leads to unnecessary arguments, conflict, and even violence in family, groups or organizations that experience more tensions and interpersonal conflicts when those affected by this syndrome are present. The educational opportunities for these persons are often disrupted and holding a job for a long time becomes almost impossible for them.

As noted above these symptoms have their roots in some previous bad experiences of discouragement, disappointment and depreciation in the lives of these youths in their formative years. There was an initially perceived injustice that led to revulsion, disgust, anger, and a feeling of being victimized.

Why are so many young black males in Belize affected by this syndrome? British expatriate and retired civil engineer, R.F. Greenwood, once asked me the proverbial question: Who taught Creole fathers to tell their sons that there was no future in Belize? The answer to that question provides some insights on the dilemma we face with many of our young black males today. We have a tendency to be simplistic when looking at the conditions of crime and poverty in Belize; we condemn the individual while overlooking the cultural influences affecting the group, but if we look at what is happening collectively with this group, the statistics verify that we are dealing with a syndrome whose roots are in the early orientations or socialization of these young boys over the last generation (1969-2009).

Why are so many black youth cynical about their future and display such a sense of hopelessness?

But it's most important area of domination was the mental universe of the colonized, the control through culture, of how people perceived themselves and their relationship to the world. Economic and political control can never be complete or effective without mental control. To control a people's culture is to control their tools of self-definition in relationship to others(10).

Again, the question: Who taught Creole fathers to tell their sons that there was no future in Belize? Who stood to gain by the acceptance of this argument and the subsequent de-peopling of young black males in Belize? Since independence black boys have killed each other in greater numbers; contracted H.I.V. in greater numbers; gone to prison in greater numbers; abandoned their children in greater numbers, and migrated to the U.S.A. in greater numbers. Who stood to gain from such a situation? Clearly we know who lost: young black males.

We have to acknowledge that for many years there was a sentiment in the hood that said: "Boay, notin no de goawn fi blackman da Belize." Translated as, nothing is going on for black men in Belize. Every personal disappointment was interpreted as evidence that this 'rule' was true. The impression was that progress was not by merit but by friends in high places and 'kisses b favor'. The system showed enough examples of disappointments and downright unfairness and cheating was known. The impression became obvious that no matter how hard you tried, as long as you were black and poor, you could not make it in Belize.

A cultural attitude grew which equated being ambitious and working hard in the system as being a 'sellout'. Distrust and cynicism was the order of the day and it became quite normal to refuse to work if working meant being paid little or nothing. Gradually, this attitude grew to become an accepted fact that there was no future for the black man in Belize and that real hope for progress was only in migrating to the U.S.A. This was the thinking in the sixties and seventies.

We are now reaping those 40 years of transformation. We have a generation of boys who have confused role models, and a cultural attitude that says nothing is fair about the system in Belize. There is no trust or loyalty in the relationships. They are "on cock" and ready for violence before violence is brought to them. They are difficult to work with and display a low trust level; suspicion clouds their every interaction. For these and other reasons, interventions programs like C.Y.D.P. and Y.F.F. have had only a superficial impact on the behavior of this sector.

However, if we want to make substantial changes in the lives of these youth our intervention must go deeper to equip them with the skills to knock that 'chip' off their shoulder.

To start with, we have to teach them how the chip got there in the first place, and in whose interest it was to have them become dysfunctional and lose hope in Belize. We have to help them explore why their fathers followed the idea that there was no future in Belize. They will also have to be taken back in time to trace the steps of the de-peopling policy that was sustained by the 'no future in Belize' argument.

They will have to understand what happens when thousands of mothers and fathers abandon their children over a sustained period of time to go to America. They have to see the connections between their anger and the socio-economic reality of their everyday life and why they have this sense of hopelessness in this complex and unfair system that exists in Belize today.

Finally, any effective program must teach these youth that the only way out of this syndrome is to establish their life compass on the unchangeable, like God, truth, justice, kindness, the golden rule, hard work and discipline, and so many other sound maxims of life that are truths regardless of space or time. It is only by building their character on unchanging principles will these youths be able to take on the long process of knocking that 'chip' off their shoulder.

# Chapter 22
# They Need Heroes

Black men in Belize have not offered young black males strong images of character to follow. This is not to say that such distinguished characters do not exist in Belize; but collectively, we have not done enough to keep these positive images in front of our youth. As black men, we have been so busy making sure that the other black man does not move out ahead of us and become a hero before we do; that we have developed the habit of tearing down and criticizing every little achievement that the next black man makes, and regrettably in this process we have cancelled out all the possible black Belizean male heroes for our young boys to emulate.

Take a minute and ask them who their heroes are and see who they come up with! Then count how many of those are black Belizean men! More than likely they would not have heard the history of men like Clifford Betson, Jamie Noguera, Telford Vernon, Charles Hyde, Horace Young, Wilhelm Arnold, C.L.B. Rogers, Edmund Martinez or Charles X Egan, and so many who were trail blazers at a time when things were far different than they are today. But even today, names like Dr. Arlie Pitters, Dr. Leroy Teager, Dr. Egbert Grinage, the pediatrician; all are modern day black Belizean heroes that most black youth have never heard of. Unfortunately their achievements and so many others are underscored and buried by our gutter-sniping habit of denying each other the honor and respect; not so much in social ceremonies where we postulate and give artificial kudos but more in our daily lives where our children observe how little respect we really show for each other's achievements.

Let's face it. We blew it. Our youths does not respect us as they should, so when we see them acting out their distorted perception of manhood in the streets of Belize City, we really should look at it in a bigger context. How did they get there? If parents and caregivers are the first line of responsibility for the rearing of the child, what method are we using to raise our children, especially boys? What kind of images we are holding in front of them to emulate?

I was recently reviewing a study/research done by David Smith in 1991/1992, examining the child rearing practices of the various ethnic groups of Belize, both in the urban and rural areas. This study, as far as I know, was never published except for some preliminary findings that were handed out by N.O.P.C.A. back in 1993. The study revealed that there are distinct patterns of child rearing among the ethnic groups of Belize influenced by historical, socio-economic and environmental factors. For example, Smith points out that the cuddling period for the Mestizo child is much longer than for the Creole child. This prolonged cuddling period where the child received continuous affirmation affected the early self-esteem of the growing child positively. Children, on the other hand, who experience continuous harsh criticism from an early age, displayed very low self-esteem.

At first glance this research would seem to suggest that Creoles are harsher with their children than Mestizos, until you take into consideration other factors, like the urban/rural divide and other socio-economic factors affecting those polled. The Creoles in the rural areas had a longer cuddling period than those polled in Belize City and as a result their children were better adjusted than those in the city. However, the Mestizos in the urban area still had a longer cuddling period than Creoles in the urban areas. Their cultural retention of parenting survived the pressures of urban living; at least at the time of this study.

Mind you this study was done nearly 20 years ago and we are living in a different social environment with a consumer oriented popular culture that affects all ethnic groups and the urban as well as the rural. While there is still a discernible divide between the urban/rural, clearly, with the introduction of cable, Internet, D.V.Ds and radio 24/7, added to the expansion of roads and instant telephone communication, all this has contributed to narrowing that divide. Therefore, the same 'virus' that affects the urban areas also affects the rural communities, to a lesser degree. But despite the fact that this study was done almost 20 years ago, what we see in Belize City today suggests that we still have childrearing patterns that are contributing to the dilemma faced by many young black males.

Some justify this situation by saying that blacks had to be tougher in preparing their children for the harsh reality of urban living therefore their children had to be toughened. But if we accept that justification don't we also have to take the responsibility for the madness we see displayed by that 'toughened' youth? Can this necessary "toughening" in our child rearing patterns be the source of some of the difficulties that some young black males have with their self-worth? In fact, no group uses the word "dis" as much as young black men -- a feeling of not being affirmed for what they perceive as their worth and therefore, feeling "disrespected". Throughout their upbringing there may not have been enough affirmation to secure their personal self-worth.

It is so out of the ordinary for black men to affirm each other that when a black man receives a compliment from another black man he instinctively becomes suspicious; "is this a setup?" It is so out of sync with our behavior with each other that we feel awkward and uncomfortable when we receive compliments and affirmation from each other. We are unsure of its sincerity. But deep down we are so starved for affirmation and acknowledgement that even those 'suspicious' ones are welcomed and sometimes make us vulnerable to manipulation as a result. Maybe this is why the crack head uses this as a strategy to get money from us as we are temporarily mesmerized by his audacious compliments.

A friend told me recently that the reason black men do not complement each other is because it will go to their head. That is like saying: I am doing you a favor when I do not acknowledge or compliment your good works; I am actually trying to save you from yourself. On the other hand, we are harsh in our criticism of each other, especially when one is not present to hear what is being said. We do not spare the rod when it comes to cutting each other down to size.

We use the Jamaican term "big up", and it is a start in affirming the good deeds of a particular person or institution; but "big up" ought to be a cultural pattern of how we relate to each other and not an occasional slang. Our conversation with each other should be imbued with positive affirmation and respect for each other's worth.

Scientists say that there are a release of the hormone endorphin in the brain when we receive complements and affirmation, and that this squirt of hormone in the brain every time we are affirmed, actually makes us feel good about ourselves and we tend to treat each other better as a result. This is not talking about 'bullshitting' someone about things that we both know is not true; but rather finding good, truthful things to say that actually improves the smooth flow of human interaction.

I started this essay reflecting on how black men have collectively dropped the ball and must therefore take responsibility for the state of young black males. I am not discarding the historical reasons that have contributed to the dysfunctions that we are seeing being played out in the socio-economic conditions of black people in Belize; but to the extent that correcting those dysfunctions are our responsibility, then more serious attention must be paid to our child rearing patterns and the kind of human being we are trying to prepare for the world. It is up to us to instill discipline in our children and point them in the direction of education as their way forward for their development.

Tina Turner sang the song: "We don't need another hero"; but I beg to differ. If there is anything that our young black boys in Belize need today its more heroes that they can emulate to work themselves out of the psychologically depressed and economically dependent conditions they find themselves in.

# Chapter 23
# Personality Disorder: As Observed Among Youths in the Criminal Justice System

Since the Y.E.A. was established in 1997 it has provided an opportunity to take a close up look at "our problem" of delinquent boys who are clogging up the criminal justice system. In the future we will be publishing the results of a psychosocial profile of over 100 of those youths that have passed through or are currently housed at the Price Barracks facility done by psycho-social worker, Olive Hampton. The results have not been all that revealing in the sense that it has confirmed what we have always known, that the majority of those in the system are from poverty, broken homes, victims of abuse, early school leavers, etc. However we will leave the result to speak for itself.

In this article we want to deal with another aspect of our observations, the problem of "personality disorder" (PD). Youths with PDs are commonly encountered within the correctional system and at YEA. Perhaps the most frequent PD displayed is 'antisocial personality disorder'; however there are a number of other maladaptive behavior patterns using the DSM III R definition of disorder(11). This overview looks at some of the most common PD patterns displayed by youths in the Belize criminal justice system; especially those who are revolving through the system as repeat offenders.

From my observation the majority of youths in prison do not display any form of real pathology. Most of their dysfunction and subsequent delinquency can be traced to a break down in the vital or sacred connections in their life, i.e. family, religious, school. Their disorder is more a reflection of a social pathology, which goes under the disguise of 'culture' or 'modern', etc, rather than individual personality disorder. However, there are some youths who display a clear mark of pathology in their perceptions of reality.

First, a word about PD. When society makes an assumption about 'order', it is referring to those values and norms that are found in the inherited tradition of that society. Referred to in the scriptures as, 'what they found their fathers doing'. These norms/mores/values, in the case of Belize, are both universal, as in the case of, 'thou shall not kill,' and local, as in the case of being considered strange to talk out loud to oneself in the middle of the Bel-China Bridge. Sometimes however, the 'order' in society changes because what may appear strange today or assumed to be a manifestation of a PD may appear to be normal decades from now because of society's change in values. For example, the half-naked styles for women today would never have been accepted in a pre-1960's Belize as "normal".

For the caregiver to be effective in treatment the question of 'disorder' versus 'order' in personality must be analyzed on an even deeper level rather than relying only on the changing value system of society. Therefore, what is normal must be seen on the basis of the original or natural man; the unchangeable characteristic of the normal personality, with all its dualities, must be identified first, before the current influences, especially those on the personality, begin to put labels on or overpower the natural man.

Now a few words on personality disorders in general. PD is very difficult to treat, because the patient has accepted that what he is and how he sees himself and the world around him is normal. It is difficult to treat someone who does not recognize that something is wrong. It is said that PD can be recognized as early as childhood and can continue throughout the life of the person. Any success at penetrating the defense mechanism and getting behind the causes for the behavior will usually cause anxiety and depression and therefore be avoided by the patient.

Here are some common PDs observed at YEA, and their symptoms:

## ANTISOCIAL PERSONALITY DISORDER(11)

Is characterized basically by continual antisocial and criminal acts but is not necessarily synonymous with criminality but is rather the inability to conform to social norms and rules.

## PARANOID PERSONALITY DISORDER(11)

It is a constant and pervasive interpretation of all actions of people as deliberately demeaning or threatening. It is usually hard to detect as a problem, since other aspects of the personality seems quite normal. It can be detected in those who have been victims of early trauma that was so drastic as to leave the impact of permanent cautiousness: "once bitten, twice shy." The paranoid often:

- Anticipates that in the end, they will lose in all actions
- Is fearful, without reason, that there is a conspiracy against him/her
- Questions the loyalty and trustworthiness of friends and associates
- Reads hidden demeaning messages into remarks only he sees
- Bears grudges and are unforgiving of insults
- Is reluctant to confide in others for fear that it may be used against him/her later

## HISTORIC PERSONALITY DISORDER(11)

Also known as hysterical personality and exhibits:

- A high degree of attention seeking behavior
- An exaggeration of thoughts and feelings and making things more important than they really are.
- Temper tantrum, tears, out bursts, if they are not the center of attention
- Constantly seeking approval which always demands reassurance/validation
- The tendency to be inappropriately sexually/seductive in appearance
- Rapidly shifting and shallow emotions
- A style of speech that is impressionistic and superficial

# NARCISSISTIC PERSONALITY DISORDER(11)

The individual:

- Has a heightened and exaggerated sense of self importance
- Displays grandiose signs of insecurities
- Consider themselves special, and is always anticipating special treatment
- Handle criticism very poorly and may become enraged
- Wants his/ her own way and can be
- Few close associates unless he is in charge
- Quite ambitious at it
- Has a fragile self-esteem and is therefore prone to depression
- Undergoes interpersonal conflicts with others over ego
- Is very physicalized in appearance and focus
- Believe that his /her problems are special and only special people understand them
- Is preoccupied with anticipating a grand success soon to come
- Requires constant attention and admiration and is always fishing for compliments
- Is unable to empathize with others unless their plight is within his /her own past experience
- Is always preoccupied with feelings of envy.

After PD has been identified in the individual there is no direct way open to change that disorder. It is very difficult to show someone something about their behavior that they have come to accept as normal. What may be diagnosed as a PD is really serving as a dam to a river of raging emotions that, if released, could come bursting forward and cause more dysfunction once you get rid of that defense line. Not only is it a long process to reach that point but the psychological re-constructive surgery necessary to come afterward just could not be done under the conditions we had to work with at YEA. Therefore, the approach used at Y.E.A. was to teach a holistic therapeutic program of human development, which helped the youths to see the model of a natural man, natural human being. From a clear image and understanding of the natural man, the youths can do his own reconstruction for self-development. By having a model of the great potential in the natural human being and what they can be if they discipline themselves, the youth go through their own transformation.

# Chapter 24
## Disrespect to Caribbean Youth

CARICOM leaders disrespected Caribbean youth when they failed to show up at the first ever CARICOM Heads of Government Special Conference on Youth, held in Paramaribo, Suriname, January 27-30, 2010. A profoundly sad message to Caribbean youth in the start of 2010, the year designated as: International Year of Youth.

The Conference was held to present a Report by the CARICOM Commission on Youth Development (C.C.Y.D.) that was mandated by CARICOM heads at their 27th meeting in 2006. Present were Dominica's Roosevelt Skerrit, St. Lucia's

Stephenson King, and host, Suriname's Runaldo Venetiaan. Guyana's President, Bharrat Jagdeo, was present for a short time.

What could have been so pressing in all these territories, simultaneously, that would have prevented nine Prime Ministers out of fourteen, from not coming to the Conference? Dominica's Dean of CARICOM Youth Ambassadors, Monelle Alexis, said that the absence of the leaders "highlighted the irony that those who purported to be gravely concerned about the future of youth and had mandated the Commission to conduct the research did not find the time to attend [the conference] to receive the Report." But this is the continuation of a pattern by Caribbean leaders who continue to give lip service to this idea of a comprehensive youth development in their territories, but who fail to make it a front burner policy initiative with the resources required.

In 2006, when the leaders called for a comprehensive report they mandated the C.C.Y.D. to conduct, "a full scale analysis of the challenges and opportunities for youth in the C.S.M.E. and to make recommendations on how to best empower them and improve their well-being." After three years the C.C.Y.D. came up with a report entitled: "Eye on the Future: Invest in YOUTH NOW for the Community Tomorrow." The report highlighted the fact that "primary school drop-out rate is staggering" throughout the region; unemployment among youth is 23% and as high as 40% in some territories; and that, at 30 per 100,000 the Caribbean has the highest murder rate in the world, and youth are the main perpetrators and primary victims. The report warns that "joblessness among youth" is a major priority for regional leaders and reminds that "there is a direct relation between joblessness and juvenile crime". The Report tabled in Suriname, formed part of the agenda at the Heads of Government intercessional meeting in March 2011, in Dominica.

One of the issues that continue to surface and was featured in press releases out of the Conference is youth involvement in the decision making process. There is no youth representation in the governance process in Belize. Whenever a youth is used they are always a token selection and not one chosen by any significant body of youth. The call for youth to have a voice in the governance process in Belize goes back to the 1980s when the first attempt was made to set up a National Youth Council (N.Y.C.). The same was being done throughout the region. There was even an attempt to set up a regional Youth Federation made up of N.Y.C. representatives from each territory that would have formed a kind of Youth CARICOM. This was headquartered in Barbados. In some territories like Barbados and Guyana there was even Mock Youth Parliament where youth sat in the National Assembly and debated issues affecting the society from a youth perspective?

Over the last twenty years these N.Y.Cs, regionally, have gone through tremendous challenges; in fact N.Y.Cs only exist as a functioning body in a few of the CARICOM states; Suriname being the "best practice". In recent years there have been repeated calls to revive these governance enhancing programs and in fact empower youth to become more proactive citizens contributing to their nation's development rather than a drain of their economies. In Belize, a serious attempt was made by Youth for the Future (Y.F.F.), in collaboration with U.N.I.C.E.F., to reactivate the N.Y.C. between 2002 and 2004. The establishment of a functional N.Y.C with youth representation from all sectors of the youth population became the major focus of the Youth Governance Unit (Y.G.U.), of the Y.F.F.

The idea of the N.Y.Cs regionally, was to provide a mechanism that allowed youth a forum to air their concerns and have a collective voice. The N.Y.C. envisioned that each sector of youth from throughout the country would have access to voice their concerns. This was more challenging for Belize, which, unlike other CARICOM states with homogeneous populations and a small land mass, was multi-cultural and multi-ethnic and spread over 8,866 sq. miles.

The N.Y.C. was to be made up of representatives from each district, while each District Council (D.C.) was made up of representatives from active youth groups from throughout the district. These D.Cs were to meet regularly with a focus on dealing with issues affecting youth in their area. At the quarterly meetings of the N.Y.C. the concerns brought from the D.Cs would be structured and position papers written and submitted to the appropriate Cabinet minister. The N.Y.Cs were to be youth advocacy groups with intent to influence government policy and to make sure issues affecting youth would remain on the front burner of policy decisions.

This vision was never fully realized because after 2004 the Y.F.F's budget was drastically cut and funding from U.N.I.C.E.F. ran out. This affected the delivery of service to this sector of youths who were just beginning to taste the idea of democracy. Despite this the Y.G.U. continued to provide empowerment training but with limited follow through. But a comprehensive youth development plan means that we end the scatter shot method of youth development that we have characterized the last thirty years. That method saw youth as an object of development initiatives rather than a subjective part of the overall development process. Or as Ms. Alexis says, "youth are a creative and valuable asset; not a problem to be solved...empower us now for the survival of the Community."

# Chapter 25
## Reflections on "Junie Balls"

George "Junie Balls" McKenzie was gunned down, gangster style, on August 27th 2007, as he exited a restaurant near Majestic Alley, an area known as his turf. A lone gunman rode up on a bicycle and fired several shots, hitting McKenzie four times, before he rode off into the dark. "Junie Balls" died on the spot: a tragic ending to one of Belize's most iconic figures in post-independence Belize. Like no other, his name was synonymous with the image of the Belizean rude boy. He had name recognition. Back in 1995, I remember being present when school children would surround Balls like some kind of hero. They were so hyped up by all the news report about "Junie Balls", that they were excited to finally see what this notorious figure looked like in person. He was charismatic and had natural communication skills. Junie Balls was an icon in his own right.

He was not a plastic or commercial rude boy but someone who had experienced the force of the Police Department who, in the early 1990s, had an 'open season' policy on destroying any presence of gang activity in Belize City. "Junie Balls" became one of their main targets. He was a symbol of gang activity in Belize City, made that way by the repeated news reports about his exploits and police actions surrounding him but also by the fact that "Junie Balls" at the time controlled a street organization which had tremendous influence on the streets of north side and significant parts of the south side of the city through a network of alliances.

This was a time when "Junie Balls", a Crip, commanded the greatest alliance that made him a powerful figure in the street world of the 1990s. He was a king on the chessboard of the streets, albeit for a short time. However, this was no enviable position – uneasy rests the head that wears the crown. On the one hand, he was hounded by the constant pressure of the police which targeted him as public enemy number one, and detained him in the 'piss house' more than twenty-five times. On the other hand, he had to deal with the turf wars: who will control the spoils of the streets? There were constant conflicts and flight was not an option for an OG. His position demanded that he faced the pains of war; the scars and the wounds; the loss of friends. He had to pay the price.

But George McKenzie yearned for more. He realized early in his kingship that he, in many ways, was a victim of circumstances, but he could not flinch from his fate. He had become head of an organization with alliances and soldiers depending on him for strength. Conflict between groups was the order of the day across the city, added to the ever present and relentless force of the police. He wanted a peace treaty just like the one he had experienced when he spent a short time in Los Angeles; where Crips and Bloods had come together to stop the violence. But there was no opening for this in Belize City; every gang was on cock and ready for action against each other.

At the time of the gang truce in 1995 there were fourteen distinct gangs operating in Belize City but their alliances fell into two colors, blue and red: Crips and Bloods. When the idea of C.Y.D.P. came along "Junie Balls" embraced it immediately and was one of the greatest voices to end gang violence through that historic truce of 1995. To show that his commitment to end the violence went beyond C.Y.D.P., even when that program was brought to an end by shortsighted politicians, "Junie Balls" did not return to his former vocation but sought to redefine himself from king pin to family man, focusing on his wife and two young sons and helping other youths through sports, especially football.

"Junie Balls" became a coach and developed several training camps for under-15 youths in football. He worked with Y.F.F. and Councilor Willoughby of the Belize City Council through summer programs in providing training for young footballers. He had a natural communication skill to motivate his trainees, and he even coached a Y.F.F. under-17 football team that won the district championship.

Unfortunately "Junie Balls" had a real problem that is still faced today by many youth like him who decide to change from a life of crime, and that is: No Way Out. How do you get out of a reputation as a rude boy once you have established it? When you have all the wannabe gangsters looking at you as the iconic, "tough rude boy", how can you turn that image around and begin to look like you are changing your image to something softer and more family-oriented? How can you go from strength to weakness; from kick ass, to kiss ass?

*"Junie Balls" (real name George McKenzie) (L) has worked for the CYDP on the Belize City Infrastructure Project for the past year. Nuri Mohammed (R), CYDP Coordinator, says Junie Balls is a prime example of a youth wanting 'to turn over a new leaf'. (21/06/96)*

This image change became a real challenge for "Junie Balls" added to the fact that he remained in the same neighborhood where all around him was the same lifestyle that he was trying to give up. Lacking in educational qualification Junior was limited in his options for meaningful employment and therefore depended on being placed in positions where he could make sufficient money, while at the same time not appearing to be a "sellout". He had a real dilemma – taking a 'average job' where he makes $150 a week, compared to the $500 a day he used to make doing what he used to do. The temptation of respect and power was constantly pulling at him. George "Junie Balls" McKenzie was going through this process when he was brutally shot down around 10 p.m. on Monday, August 27, 2007.

# Chapter 26
# Why Hungry Children 40 Years Later?

Forty years ago, a group of young radicals tried to address the hunger problem of school children in Belize City by initiating a Free Breakfast Program. The program was modeled off a similar initiative started by the Black Panther Party in California in the mid 1960s. This program had as its objective, providing a nutritious breakfast to poor children to ensure that they could function properly in school. It is amazing that forty years later we are still dealing with the issue of poor nutrition for school children.

In 1994, Dr. Cardio Martinez, a pediatrician attached to the Karl Heusner Memorial Hospital (K.H.M.H.) informed me that he was alarmed about the amount of malnourished children that he observed in his care. He noted that there was a crisis of malnourished children who would obviously be affected later in their lives because of a lack of proper nutrition stemming from their prenatal stage. He lamented that malnutrition has a debilitating effect on the brain function of a developing child and that stunted physical growth was only one aspect of the problem. Dr. Martinez stated that the other even larger problem is the mental aptitude of these children when they enter school. He noted at the time that there was no concerted effort to address this problem in any coordinated way, and that Belize would pay for it because we will have thousands of dysfunctional children whose condition is rooted in malnourishment. That was 19 years ago the doctor told me that.

Over the years we have seen several efforts to create feeding programs in a number of schools; some have been successful while others have not effectively mitigated the crisis. There are still thousands of hungry children going to school in Belize City and different parts of the country. Forty years ago, the Breakfast Program was an initiative launched by the United Black Association for Development (U.B.A.D.). While little or no mention of this innovative program has been highlighted during the continuous recollection of U.B.A.D's history, it was an idea way before its time. It started when I suggested to the leaders of U.B.A.D. that we launch a program to address a pressing need affecting poor people in the city. The idea was accepted and preparation was made to gather donations of foodstuff from local merchants like Brodie's, Castillo and Ishmael Gomez. Then it was getting a place to serve the breakfast. We first approached the Minister of Local Government at the time, Mr. Hector Silva, who supported the idea but he could not get the support of his Cabinet colleagues. The Cabinet apparently saw it as an embarrassment to the government since it suggested that there were "starving children in Belize." It was also very concerned with the ambitions of these young radicals and was determined not to give support to further their cause.

The key players on that team of young radicals were: Eleanor Gill (aka Vernon), Lillette Barkley Waite, Penny Cassasola, Charles Stamp, Jeff Scott, Galento Neal, Lionel 'Bakatown' Mathews, Karl Menzies, Odinga Lumumba and this writer. Despite the obstacles in finding a place the young radicals decided to use the U.B.A.D. headquarters on Hyde's Lane. The sisters got up early to prepare the breakfast while the rest of us circled the city in a Willy's Jeep to pick up the children. When the government saw that we were determined to go ahead despite their refusal to help, they made their second move to stop the program by preventing me from driving the jeep because it was not insured in my name.

My friend Mike Allen, a white American who owned the Jeep, then began to pick up the children. This must have infuriated the authorities that despite their effort to stop the program, we kept going. Then came the final move by government. Using a police detachment headed by the late Corporal Gideon, they arrested Mike and drove him up to the Corozal/Mexico border and deported him; stamping in his passport: persona non grata. That effectively killed the program. We tried to continue using taxis but that was not effective and the program eventually came to an end.

What was done 40 years ago was just a spontaneous effort by some youths to address a visible problem of malnutrition and its effects on our children. There was no intent to embarrass the government, but more an effort to turn our talk of "serving the people" into action. The government, in crushing the program, showed their short-sightedness. Feeding hungry children should have never been allowed to become a political issue. Imagine what would have happened if that government had embraced these young radicals and allowed them to channel their youthful energies into this worthwhile cause. Maybe today there would be no need for a second "Height Census" to determine how many children "down-grow" because of malnutrition.

Kudos to the Amandala Editorial of Wednesday May 13, 2009 which highlighted, in eloquent terms, the gravity of the situation of our hungry children, and made some practical suggestions to address this very solvable embarrassment to our country.

# Chapter 27
## Avoiding Dependency

Belize is truly fortunate that some of the racial hostility that exists between ethnic groups in other countries does not exist here to the same degree, despite our ethnic diversity. However, we are not naive enough to pretend that no tension or prejudice exists between groups but presently it is still at a minimum and we should all do our part to keep Belize free of racial hostility.

But while race as a basis for prejudice and discrimination is not prevalent in Belize classism and the varied assumptions that go along with it are there. A friend told me he witnessed an interesting incident recently. This Mestizo mother was telling her son to stop acting like "den Southside boy." Obviously his mannerism and demeanor reminded his mother of a behavior that she didn't approve of, and one she associated with a certain class of people from a certain section of Belize City. While this is not directly racism it is easy to see how it can get that interpretation if we do not understand the context out of which that mother spoke.

In a column I wrote some time ago I noted that many young black males in Belize, and to an extent black men, depended too much on the 'victim card' when trying to get a job, a loan or a scholarship, or just sympathy for their situation. In other words, "help me because I am a victim". My point was that there are many people who come from equally disadvantageous backgrounds who are not relying on any handout to make it; they take life as they find it and are doing the best they can to survive. In other words they refuse to play the 'victim card.'

This 'victim card' is not exclusively use by young black males but in fact it is an established strategy for correcting perceived injustices within a system. A perfect example is the 'Affirmative Action' (A.A.) approached used in the U.S.A. to correct years of unequal treatment of blacks in that country. The rationale for A.A. was that blacks should be given special consideration over whites in jobs, education, housing, etc., in order to correct the years that blacks had been deprived of equal justice in every aspect of civil rights in that country. As a result of the A.A. policy many American blacks have received a jump-start (a kind of skip to the front of the line) support to correct the historical built-in injustice in the US system.

Women in the US have also used the 'victim card' to highlight the fact that some kind of A.A. should exist to address the injustices built into the system that deprive women of equal rights. There are many other examples of where the 'victim card' was appropriate as a strategy to correct systemic injustices.

The most internationally known use of the victim card has been its use by the European Jews. Historically they have used the victim card as an effective strategy for advancing their status as a Jewish nation. With the creed: "Never again", they have etched into the world's consciousness stories of the atrocities that was done to them in Europe during World War II and as a result they have garnered world sympathy for their plight as a people. While other groups people have suffered similar or worse atrocities the narrative of the Jewish genocide in Germany is most predominant in the world's consciousness and is often used as the prime example of "man's inhumanity to man". Similarly, their narrative of the Jewish state of Israel being surrounded by "aggressive Arab states" is another example of their effective use of the 'victim card' strategy.

So the use of the victim card is nothing new. The problem with using the 'victim card' comes when a person feels they have a right over others by virtue of the fact that they have gone through what others have not. When you begin to depend on sympathy to justify that you should be helped before others then you are caught in the trap of victimology. This is where the 'victim card' becomes a problem in Belize. We don't have a history of systemic injustice directed at a specific group, and therefore we have no justification for an A.A. type approach to our problem of prejudice and discrimination.

Clearly the statistics are revealing that many of our black male youths are falling through the cracks and need special interventions to address their peculiar socioeconomic problems but including the 'victim card' in the equation or as the basis of our intervention, is not the best approach. For example, there are many beggars in the city today; some are clearly victims and need a hand out to pull them through their temporary hard times till things get better for them, while others have decided to turn begging into a daily profession. Despite their unfortunate circumstances others have decided to turn their misfortune into an opportunity to work their way out of their dilemma. Who do you think will get the most support, the perpetual victim or the one who is asking for help to help themselves?

It is almost becoming an accepted fact now that black men in Belize City are lazy and want everything for free. Despite its derogatory nature this is a growing opinion among many who cite all kinds of examples to verify their point. They say, look how the Chinese, Indians and Arabs own all the stores that black Belizeans once owned. Look how the new Belizeans from Central America have established themselves over the last twenty-five years. They say, unlike the new Belizeans, if you offer a black man in the city a job he is more concerned about how much he will make, and if the price is not right he would prefer to be without a job than to work for below what he considers his value. This may sound like a generalization but you make your own anecdotal observation of these matters and see what we are dealing with. We have developed a culture of dependency in Belize where to be a perpetual victim is becoming commonplace for many young males.

We all know that working hard and working smart is the key for survival especially in this depressed economy that we face in Belize today. But how many are waiting for the "right" job before they will accept any job? How many are satisfied to stand on the sidelines and complain instead of getting out there and find a job, and failing that, making one? The fact is there are many legal ways to generate an income, albeit small, but such jobs have no glitter attached to them; they may be dirty and backbreaking and pay below the minimum wage but they can sustain you till you find something better.

They say that 'necessity is the mother of invention' and that there are lights at the end of every dark tunnel; but if you do not live in a culture that encourages you to work with what you have and to not become dependent on someone to do for you what you can do for yourself, you will miss many opportunities to improve your situation.

Constantly crying about the half empty glass and failing to acknowledge what assets you have to work with eventually kills creativity and renders you forever dependent. We have all heard the story of the man who prayed vehemently to G-d to bless him with shoes because he had none. He became vexed in spirit because his prayers went unanswered until one day he met a man who had no feet but was yet cheerful and productive. Clearly this man experienced an epiphany and at that moment learned the importance of working with what you have to make it.

It is the responsibility of government to stimulate an enabling environment where jobs are created both in the public and well as private sector. A good government targets the employment of its citizens as a top priority; however, if jobs are not readily available then the individual has to find his own way and avoid dependency.

# Chapter 28
## Not without Money

Thomas Jefferson used the word "twistification" to describe a dilemma that arises in a democracy where the ideals of the republic are in conflict with the reality of the everyday life of ideas that define that democracy. No doubt in the infancy of our democracy in Belize we are beginning to notice some anomalies that are in stark contradiction to what we say we are about, at least, what our Constitution says we are about. It is clear that we too must look at our own "twistification" in our democracy that we so proudly proclaim.

While we know that there is a constitutional proposition that proclaims: 'Equality before the law', this is not always the case because of the way our legal system works. This is not a critique of the Judiciary because this is not where the real problem lies. The Judiciary, especially the decisions coming from the Chief Justice in the last six years, has given a sense of confidence in the integrity of the courts. The problem lies in the question of access of the average citizen to the courts and especially the highest court in the land, the Supreme Court.

Regardless of what law has been passed by the National Assembly, if any Belizean feels aggrieved by the execution of that law, they have a right to challenge that law. This is a right guaranteed us by our Constitution. The problem is money. If you do not have the money to pay for the legal fees to launch the challenge you do not really have access to redress through the courts. So in reality, while you may have a perfectly legitimate case where your constitutional rights are being violated, if you do not have the money to get legal representation to fight for your rights your perfectly legitimate case can go uncontested.

The legal system unfortunately is set up for the rich and not for the poor. Sure the poor can get their day in court but in most cases it is to get themselves free of some charge levied against them rather than them launching a challenge to the violation of their constitutional rights. There are so many examples as in the Crime Control Act where the constitutional right of the citizen can be challenged, but without redress the illegal measures become enshrined in the proclivities of the law(6).

The constitutional right to work, for example, was violated in 2009 when this government fired workers because of their political affiliation. The Constitution protects a citizen's "right to work" and it guarantees the right to "freedom of association". If a person is fired because of politics this is grounds for a constitutional challenge. In other words, those who were fired could have formed themselves into an ad hoc group and brought a class action suit against the government to challenge the violation of their constitutional right; but without a legal team to launch the challenge those workers rights remained violated without legal redress.

Another example is the Government's recent attempt to put in place legislative provisions to muzzle the unions in the name of "essential services". This was a classic case of constitutional violation that could have been challenged through the court with a sure win in favor of the unions; but without the necessary challenge the proposed adjustment in the law stood.

While we claim to have constitutional rights within this system the truth is that this is a system where those who have money can protect their rights while those without must suffer constitutional abuse. Take the classic case of the Crimes Control Act I & II that gives the police the right to enter private property without a warrant or some form of judicial review(6). The constitutional protection against "arbitrary search and entry" is clearly enshrined in the constitution to guarantee that citizens would be safe from unwarranted violation of their rights. If authorities have enough plausible evidence then let them subject it to judicial review and get the appropriate warrant to search that citizen;

but through the application of these Acts the constitutional guarantees have been suspended giving license to violation of citizen's rights by authorities that have been given a free hand without fear of reprimand.

These Acts, under the guise of protecting society against the evil of drugs and weapons, have given the police the right to stop and search or enter the property of any citizen they randomly choose. Certainly we must all agree that the most stringent measures must be put in place to combat the scourge of drugs and weapons and their impact on our society; and the police must be empowered with all the weapons and facilities necessary to combat this social enemy. But this emotional allowance on the part of us the citizenry should not be taken for granted by police authorities, and therefore give license to renegade cops who feel free to do as they please and to violate the rights of innocent citizens in the process without any fear of reprimand. If these cases were taken before the Supreme Court many would be found unjustified and unconstitutional, but the Acts protect the police against any charge of violation of citizen's rights.

When the late Sir Barry Bowen felt that his constitutional right was being violated by sections of the Sixth Amendment he sued and won a case against the actions of the Executive. His access to the Court was contingent on his ability to afford redress. Without money he would have been subjected to this provision just like the rest of us; but with the wherewithal to launch a legal and constitutional challenge to the government for his rights he kept our democracy alive. The fact, however, is that this basic principle is being violated in so many other ways that are not brought to light, because those who are violated lack legal representation.

The case of the Maya's challenge to government regarding their land rights serves as another unique case study. Here was an alliance of Mayan leaders who came together to sue the government to guarantee the respect for their peculiar claim over land. The Court ruled that the Belize Constitution gives recognition and respect to the peculiar customs of people living in Belize, especially if those customs are rooted in ancestral practice. It says that the constitution recognizes that those customary rights are to be valued and respected. The important issue here, however, is that the Maya leaders were well funded from foreign sources in their efforts to challenge the government. Again this makes the point that without funds to launch a legal challenge the rights of the average citizen is compromised despite our claim of: equality before the law.

A lot must be said about that special class of lawyers who have taken up cases pro bono to bring redress to the Court on these constitutional issues for the poor and un-established. Kudos to Lisa Shoman, Anthony Sylvester, Kevin Arthurs and Antoinette Moore and other attorneys who are in the forefront of confronting the government on application of laws that violate constitutional principles. There is need for more "human rights" attorneys to take up the challenge and ensure that our system is based on the principles of our Constitution.

Another area where this inequality shows up is the use of judicial review that seems to have been reserved for high profile cases, but is actually a provision in our Constitution open to any citizen that feels aggrieved by a matter that is to be brought before the Court. The problem is that only the rich have the access to challenge the charge leveled against them; therefore money continues to be the important factor in our justice system.

How do we deal with this anomaly in our justice system? We say that the Legal Aid Center can alleviate the problem, but we know that they can only deal with minor cases and are not equipped to take on Supreme Court cases that mean that the issue of redress to the higher court is left unresolved. We need to provide some form of access to the ordinary citizen to have access to the Courts to challenge those cases that violate their constitutional rights. At this point in our history we only provide the rich access to the High Court by virtue of the high cost of legal fees to challenge laws that violate the constitutional right of every citizen.

Recently in its 16 Days of Activism the Women's Department featured an innovative idea of a one-day legal clinic where the ordinary citizen could access legal information that they would normally have to pay exorbitant fees for. For a day, citizens were offered free legal advice on how to access the legal system and to seek redress for the numerous challenges that face them. While the main focus of this day clinic was domestic abuse and other gender issues there is room to expand this concept and include a clinic that provides access for the average of us to get legal redress. This is an idea that could be expanded on and with the collaboration of the Bar Association there could be an on-going provision of service to the ordinary Belizean who needs access to legal service.

The Ombudsman is also empowered with the legal provisions to provide access to the higher courts for the average citizen that feels aggrieved. The Ombudsman should be a starting point for taking up such cases, but as far as I know that office only deals with complaints of a civil nature and thus far there has never been a constitutional challenge to any law coming from the Ombudsman.

# Chapter 29
# Crisis for Whom?

The Cabinet has announced that crime has reached crisis proportion in Belize. When the highest governing body, the Cabinet, declares that there is a crisis the whole nation is consumed and the crisis becomes a national one. According to the dictionary a crisis is "a situation that has reached an extremely difficult or dangerous point...requiring immediate action to address it." But what defines our crisis? Where is it located? It is a crisis for whom? All these questions come up when we hear the grand announcement of a "crisis".

Before we examine our current crisis let us remember that we have been down this path several times before. It was a crisis in 1990 that gave rise to the bi-partisan Crime Commission of 1992 with its many recommendations. Again, it was the gang crisis of 1995 that gave birth to the C.Y.D.P.; and again, there was a crisis in 2002 that led to Y.F.F. Each time we responded out of crisis; but while a crisis can be a useful catalyst for implementing transformational changes, if programs coming out of that crisis are not sustained for the long haul, then we will continue to return to the ever-present crisis point.

Let us look at the current crisis and ask again: crisis for whom? Certainly we know that it must be a crisis for the government whose reputation for managing crime is at stake. It is also a crisis for those neighborhoods, especially Lake Independence, Collet and Port Loyola, where the majority of the city's violent crimes occur. But beyond that parameter where is the crisis? There are clustered communities even within Belize City itself that rarely experience the impact of the crisis because they are well off enough to buffer themselves from the epicenter of crime, and may not feel the crisis any at all. There are parts of King's Park, Hone Park, seaside residents, University Heights area, Buttonwood Bay; these are areas where the noise of the "crisis" is rarely heard. Folks in these areas live a distance from the crisis.

Another example is that those who live in the rural areas of Belize, which accounts for over half of our population. To them, crime in Belize City may be as far away as a C.N.N. International Report, but because of their organic connection with Belize City they feel a concern, but not urgency, about the crisis. Rural villagers sleep quietly at night, never a concern about gunshots or the sound of sirens from police or ambulances, like in the city. But why does not everybody take the Cabinet crisis, as a crisis? It is because not everybody feels affected by crime as it is defined on the south side of Belize City. The death of Aubrey Lopez brought crime close to home for many but apparently still not close enough. We live in such a scattered and diverse demographic in Belize that crime is still distant for many of us.

Aubrey Lopez's murder is the stark reality that crime is moving up the mobility scale. With Aubrey, middle and upper class Belizeans must now take notice because it could have been their son, husband, father, nephew, brother, cousin, friend. It was not until the sons and daughters of United States Senators and Congressmen became the victims of the drug inspired crime crisis in the U.S.A. that their government began to pay attention back in the 1980s. Maybe Aubrey will be our cross-over point in Belize and the death of this upstanding, middle class, teacher and basketball player will be that catalyst. But the real challenge is the way forward. What strategy will this Cabinet use to combat this scourge of crime that has propelled us to "crisis" again?

## HERE IS A FORMULA FOR THE WAY FORWARD TO BE CONSIDERED BY THE CABINET.

First there needs to be a Commission of Crime Eradication (C.C.E.) empowered to control and eventually eliminate crime in Belize City in the following four quadrants:

The first quadrant is already in operation with a show of "occupational" force in hot spots of the City. This quadrant is reactive by nature to the crisis at hand and the need to signal to citizens that security forces are in place to prevent the occurrence of street violence that have resulted from rival youth conflicts. The second benefit of this quadrant is the presence on the ground of lethal forces to deter the wayward youth from criminal activities. This is especially effective in the Port Loyola area and serves as a major deterrence. **Quadrant I** must of necessity be heavy handed to discourage criminals from ever wanting to get caught up in the criminal system again. Quadrant I should be an "ugly realty check"; one they will not forget.

**Quadrant II** is long range in scope and is aimed at intervention with leaders and shot callers among the target population to engage them in innovative approaches to addressing the problem of youth crime and violence, and enable initiatives that come from these disenfranchised youth to be activated. This quadrant should be staffed with qualified individuals using innovative ways to redirect the negative energy of gang violence to productive self development and development of the society in general. Kind of what a C.Y.D.P. should have been doing.

**Quadrant III** must also be long range in scope. It recognizes that the manifestation of youth crime and violence has its roots in far deeper socio-economic paradigms that have affected Belize since independence and before. Quadrant III recognizes that the issue of crime is rooted in those social constructs of disparity and inequality and corrective measures must be put in place to curtail the perpetual inequalities and return justice to the system. Quadrant III, therefore, is concerned with preventing criminality by putting in place structures that mitigate the tendency of poor youths to be involved with crime. Quadrant III is preventative in nature and works to stop crime before it becomes a social menace. Using already existing training units like the Institute for Technical Vocational Education and Training (I.T.V.E.T.) and other institutions, this Quadrant seeks to empower youths to become productive and provide for them. Youth enterprise and small business development are useful tools in this Quadrant, and would be best coordinated by the Ministry of Economic Development.

**Quadrant IV** deals with the big picture and addresses the popular cultural climate that encourages crime and criminality in the population, especially youths. Not all those with criminal intent commit crimes but the propensity for crime has increased because of a popular culture that condones criminality. Quadrant IV is focused on exposing and changing that popular culture that encourages and supports crime. Crime does not take place in a vacuum and those who commit criminal acts many times feel justified by a popular culture that justifies certain types of crime. While murder, rape and child molestation remain universal no-no's, crimes like theft, robbery, handling stolen goods, and drug trafficking are all crimes that have been justified and found normal in the genre of popular culture.

So Quadrant IV has to be focused on challenging popular culture and offering alternatives that justify that it is better to do the right thing. Quadrant IV has to make doing the right thing attractive. There are some infomercials from the "Foundation for a Better Life" that shows "doing the right thing" can be very attractive. Quadrant IV should be coordinated by a body like the National Institute of Culture and History (N.I.C.H.) which can bring together the whole culture community of Belize to work on the development of a new, positive youth culture.

Quadrant IV is also where the religious community, if they are serious, can be most effective in their actions against crime. The gems of religious teachings must be presented to youth as a dynamic approach to life that gives them control over their decisions for their future. Religious teachings should be an attractive alternative to a life of crime. Religious leaders should be an important resource within Quadrant IV.

All of these quadrants must be implemented simultaneously and sustained individually, while being in concert with the other. This will be the role of the C.C.E. The coordination of these activities within the four quadrants will avoid duplication and encourage shared resources within the separate quadrants.

The objective of this essay was to share some ideas on the way forward in dealing with the issue of youth, crime and violence. This is not a new problem. We have been down this road before and if we remain in our current mindset we will no doubt return to this juncture of crisis several times to come. This essay suggests some immediate actions that can break the cycle and move to coordinated and concerted action to better manage Belize's number one problem: crime.

# Chapter 30
# Robin Hood: A Recurring Saga in Criminal Enterprise

One of the questions asked by observers of the tragedy that unfolded in Tivoli Gardens, West Kingston, Jamaica in late May 2010, is whether Christopher "Dudus" Coke, was seen as a Robin Hood by residents of the area who were so willing to give their lives to protect him from government security forces bent on extraditing him to the U.S.A. to face charges of narco-trafficking, money laundering and weapons charges.

Robin Hood, as he has come down in legend, is a medieval English outlaw who controlled Sherwood Forest, an area just outside the gates of the King's castle in Fourteenth Century England. Robin's fame grew because he robbed the rich nobles as they travelled to and from the castle, and used the wealth to feed the poor serfs who lived in the villages surrounding the castle. This romantic story about a benevolent criminal formed a part of early European folklore and spawned many minstrels with ballads and operas that kept the tale alive.

In the early part of the last century Hollywood became fascinated with the myth and produced many films with the swashbuckling Robin played by such stars like Douglas Fairbanks, Errol Flynn and so many others. In fact, Robin Hood is one of the most played characters in movie history. Despite the popularity of the character these films only focused on the superficial, romantic aspects of Robin and his merry men, and never touched the socio-political aspects of the story -- the fact that he robbed from the rich to feed the poor. But while Hollywood may not have played up that part

*Insights into Gang Culture in Belize – Stray Thoughts*

of the Robin Hood legend many modern day criminals have seen their story in the myth of Robin Hood.

One such notorious criminal was Pablo Escobar of Colombia. He was known as the "padrino" of the region from which he ran his Medellin cartel. He saw himself as a kind of Robin Hood and rationalized his criminal enterprise as a means of sustenance for the poor and underserved people who depended on his generosity for their survival in a region where the Colombian government was ineffective.

The Armed Revolutionary Forces of Colombia (F.A.R.C.) and the Movimiento 19 de April (M-19) also saw themselves in the cloak of a Robin Hood. Their involvement in narco-trafficking in the 1980s and 1990s had an ideological rationale to it and was not seen as a means of personal gain and enrichment for the few, but as a means of buying the resources to sustain their guerrilla war against the Colombian government and the establishment of a "people's government"

Jamaican journalist, Bernard Headley, points out in his book "Essays on Crime and the Politics of Jamaica"(12), that it would be a mistake to compare Jamaican drug lords with narco-trafficking done by the groups like the F.A.R.C. and M-19, since in the case of Jamaican drug lords there was "no hint of a larger political or ideological intent, such as overthrowing the Government or bringing down any of its institutions. Illegal gain is the only game, and moving and selling drugs is the only agenda."

Despite the absence of a 'rich against poor' ideology among Jamaican drug lords, in the matrix of Jamaica's socio-political landscape the criminal enterprise ran by the dons have interwoven itself into the livelihood of the people who surround the communities where the criminal organizations exist. In Tivoli Gardens, which is known for its massive unemployment, poor access to health care and education, limited access to potable water and poor sanitation, "Dudus" Coke operated two legitimate businesses; one, Incomparable Enterprise, which received millions in state contracts; and two, Presidential Click, an entertainment company and promoter of the country's largest street parties and musical events. Both companies provided employment for hundreds of residents of the area. Coke's organization also built medical and community centers, paid school fees, gave scholarships and paid hospital bills. Coke's contribution to the community's development earned him the reputation of a Robin Hood in the eyes of the residents who showed their willingness to make his fight theirs.

Belize has not yet developed the kind of criminal organization that exists in Jamaica for a number of reasons. The closest Belize came to the mythical Robin Hood character was the late George "Junie Balls" McKenzie. McKenzie never developed a sophisticated criminal operation like the Shower Posse, as did Coke, but that has to do more with the political as well as the criminal history of the two countries. McKenzie was a first generation gangster, while Coke is a second generation coming from a father, Lester Lloyd "Jim Brown" Coke, who was responsible for the transformation of the Shower Posse from a Jamaica Labor Party, get-out-the-vote community organization, to a multi-million dollar transnational drugs and arms running operation that stretched from Jamaica to New York, Miami and London. So influential was the older Coke in the politics of Jamaica that when he died mysteriously in a fire while in Jamaican custody in 1992, the then leader of the Jamaica Labour Party, Edward Seaga, walked in front of his funeral.

*Insights into Gang Culture in Belize – Stray Thoughts*

So while compared to Coke, McKenzie's enterprise was considered "small time," there was a similarity in character they shared in the saga of Robin Hood. McKenzie was seen as a "padrino" to many youth around him even though he was only in his twenties. He was generous and made sure that he took care of those in need. As a result, his funeral a few years ago was one of the largest in Belize City attended by many poor people who had no criminal connection to McKenzie. The saga of Robin Hood has lasted more than seven hundred years and continues to inspire criminals who use his prototype as a justification for their enterprise with the motto: rob from the rich to feed the poor.

# Chapter 31
# Return of the Quick Trial Court?

According to an unconfirmed media report in September 2011 the Police intended to set up a "Special Court" to strengthen its prosecutorial branch. When I first read this I thought that this sounds like the return of a strategy tried by this U.D.P. government back in 1994 when faced with a similar crime crisis like today where the magistracy is gridlocked because of the overwhelming amount of cases grinding through the system. They introduced the Quick Trial Court back then, whose objective was to fast forward as many high profile, criminal youths to prison as possible. The magistracy had become clogged up with cases and the system was not functioning effectively. With the upsurge of those in detention, caused by the increased powers of the police to arrest under the Crimes Control Act, the Courts became overwhelmed thus the justification for an "extra-judicial" measure called the Quick Trial Court(6).

However, that time around the motivation was different, according to the then Commissioner of Police, Crispin Jefferies. This "Special Court" will fall under the protocols of the magistracy, and will not be a constitutional breach as some believed. "It will not bypass the constitutional authority of the Director of Public Prosecution's (D.P.P.) Office, but will target selected cases passing through the system".

For years there has been a problem with the collaboration between the police and the Office of the D.P.P. The D.P.P's office has complained that the police are not thorough in their case preparation and proper documentation of evidence, and that there is lack of skilled personnel at the Police Prosecution Branch, with some police prosecutors having only a high school diploma coming up against trained attorneys. That disconnect between the police and the D.P.P's office seems to be endemic, prompting the Chief Justice to add his voice to the serious concerns about the failure in the prosecutorial process. This animosity between these two offices goes back to several D.P.Ps and Commissioners of Police; and it is said that there is no love lost between the two current holders of those offices. This is a dilemma faced in the criminal justice system for some time. While the police are effective in identifying, in most cases, the guilty, the problem is how to get the guilty to be found 'legally guilty'?

The attention necessary for wining these winnable cases is grossly lacking at the bridge that connects the police to the D.P.P's office in preparing cases for prosecution. The recent beefing up of its prosecutorial section by hiring Elizabeth Purcell as a Police Crown Counsel is one attempt to correct this major breach, according to the Commissioner. With a trained legal mind involved in the process from arrest to prosecution, the police are hoping to improve its dismal record of 7% prosecution in 2010. But when looked at in a broader perspective any return to a fast track strategy in the judiciary is only a continuation of dealing with the symptom and not the root of the problem of crime.

The catastrophic oil spill that occurred in the Gulf of Mexico a few years ago provides a lesson for those who want to fight crime in Belize in a systemic way. The objective in dealing with that massive oil spill in the Gulf was twofold, first, to stop the source of the spill polluting the area; and second, to clean up or "restore" the area damaged by the spill. While quantum efforts were made to mitigate the impact of the spill on the livelihood of the residents of the coastline and the effects on the wildlife in the area, the bigger problem was stopping the source of the spill. Without addressing the source first, the restoration effort would have been endless. Belize is faced with a similar dilemma as we deal with crime and violence. We have launched many programs to mitigate the impact of crime but very few were directed at capping the source of the crime crisis itself.

A few columns back I provided the outline of a crime fighting strategy in which I divided the scope of the work into four Quadrants, I, II, III and IV. Quadrant I could be called the clean-up response to the spill, such as Operation Jaguar and Restore Belize, while Quadrants II, III, and IV would be an attempt to cap the source of the spill.

Quadrants II, III and IV are long range in scope and should be aimed at capping the leak that keeps us coming back to crisis point every few months. They should be aimed at intervention with leaders and shot callers among the target population to engage them in innovative approaches and enable initiatives that come from these disenfranchised youth. These quadrants should use innovative ways to redirect the negative energy of gang violence to productive self-development and macro-development of the society in general. Quadrants II, III and IV should recognize that the manifestation of youth crime and violence has its roots in far deeper socio-economic paradigms that have affected Belize since independence and before. These quadrants recognize that the issue of crime is rooted in those social constructs of disparity and inequality, and corrective measures must be put in place to curtail the perpetual inequalities and return justice to a system that is failing. These quadrants, therefore, are concerned with preventing criminality by putting in place structures that mitigate the tendency of poor youths to be involved with crime. They are preventative in nature and work to stop crime before it becomes a social menace.

The most effective long range deterrent against crime is EDUCATION; the second is INCOME-GENERATION. Using already existing training units like the I.T.V.E.T. and other institutions, these quadrants seek to empower youths to become productive and self-sufficient. Youth enterprise and small business development are useful tools in these quadrants. Quadrant II, III and IV deal with the big picture and addresses the popular cultural climate which is a major source of the spilling of criminal minds into our society. This culture encourages crime and criminality in the population, especially youths. Not all those with criminal intent commit crimes but the propensity for crime has increased because of this popular culture that condones criminality, if one can get away with it. These quadrants must focus on exposing and changing this popular culture. Crime does not take place in a vacuum and those who commit criminal acts many times feel justified by a rational that encourages ideas like, 'cover your bases' and 'don't let your right hand know what your left hand is doing'.

So these quadrants, if implemented, can work towards the capping of the spill that continues to produce criminals like a gushing leak into the Belizean population. They must focus on challenging the popular culture and offer alternatives that justify that it is better to do the right thing. These quadrants have to make doing the right thing attractive. As I outlined in the original column all of these quadrants must be implemented simultaneously and sustained individually, while being in concert with each other. This would be the role of a Coordination Unit, to avoid duplication and to share resources. "Restore Belize" seems to have adapted some of these ideas; however their Coordination Unit still appears to be burdensome and bureaucratic, which in government spells: 'no progress.'

# Afterword

As I said in the introduction, this book was not an attempt to impress the reader with impractical research backed up by statistical data, rather this is an expression of deep concern from one who speaks from a close up, antidotal observation of this sector of our population over the last thirty years. There is, however, a great need for formal research to be done on the antecedents of this phenomenon so that programs and projects are more properly targeted to reach desired goals. This is where tertiary level institutions and NGOs can play a major role in providing quantitative analysis of the problem before money is spent on ineffective, knee-jerk, reactionary programs.

Since the time of the first essay in this book (1992) the whole gang phenomenon has mushroomed, and like a virus, has transformed itself into a new strain that is resistant to the old methods used to control its initial spread. Today we are dealing with a more complex configuration of this subgroup than twenty three years ago; then it was about colors and turf, today it is about raw power fueled by ego, ignorance and the proceeds from the drug trade. Ego mixed with ignorance is a recipe for violence, especially when alcohol is involved.

In a recent report cited in the September 6, 2015 edition of the Amandala, titled, "Murder rates rising sharply in many U.S. cities", New Orleans police superintendent, Michael Harrison, said the rise in homicides in his city "did not appear to reflect any increase in gang violence....but by people who know their victims.....it speaks to a culture of violence deeply ingrained in a community – a segment of the population where people are resolving their problems in a violent way". I am sure that if such a study was done in Belize it would find a similar shifting trend in the occurrence of violence in Belize. There have been reported cases of fights started over Facebook posting.

While scarcity of money has drawn these youth into the network of the drug trade the problem is further complicated by the psycho-social and spiritual factors already apparent with this sector. As we have tried to make clear in these essays our approach to addressing the problem must be more holistic, inclusive of the psychological, educational, and employment aspects and not confine only to policing.

The criminal culture has become entrenched in Belize, not only at the bottom of the pyramid where most of the reported and prosecuted crimes take place, but clearly the revelations of corruption in high places in recent years is evidence that the crime culture is not contained in one area. Belize is a small fish-bowl society where everybody knows each other's businesses; and as the song says: 'The night has a thousand eyes'.

Therefore, crime must be seen first as a moral problem that has become a major social cancer. Crime is justified not only by the one that does the actual criminal act but also by those who silently or indirectly support it. Take the good father who buys a laptop off the streets because he wants to help his daughter in college who needs a computer. He is a good father, and he knows by his purchase he is a part of the criminal network, but he justifies it. How about the pawnshop owner who accepts a piece of expensive jewelry from somebody he knows can't afford it, then turns around and make a profit in the resale. Or the business person who makes an 'under the table' deal with a Customs official to avoid paying high import duties. All are connected to the criminal culture. This collective moral justification or rationalization for wrong is where the culture of crime takes root. It thrives in an atmosphere of relativity, of double standard that says: "do as I say not as I do", or "don't let your right hand know what your left hand is doing" – all these contribute to a weak moral environment where crime breeds. Belize has to deal with this gangster culture.

Rooting out crime in Belize today is not as easy as we think; if we want to see any meaningful change in curtailing its spread we must all take personal responsibility. We must feel that we have something to do with what is happening around us. In small ways we must recognize the criminal culture and do what is available at our disposal at the time to do something to change it, or to speak out against it or just express our utter disgust with its presence in our community. It's only when the criminal culture is seen as death and degradation in the community that our youth will begin to disengage from it. It presently is an attraction to them because there is no attractive alternative but if that alternative is placed in front of them they would choose "better" over "worst".

So what is the alternative that we have to put in front of them? Certainly it can't' be the same ole same ole. We need a preparedness program that will equip these youth to be productive citizens in the overall development of the country. We need to empower them by putting the wheels of their development process in their hands. We as elders have to redefine our role from being in charge, or the "boss", to being the support for their leadership. We have to be their institutional memory and allow them to recover from mistakes in their learning process.

As alarming as having the infamous reputation of being one of the most murderous countries in the world, Belize is far from lost. We are very far from lost. Our cancer is not malignant. There are great possibilities for remission if we are decisive. I leave you with the hope that we can be.

# Terms used by Gangs in Belize

Many of these terms have their origins in the cities of the U.S and the Caribbean, but have been creolized locally. While many of them are used by gang affiliates, they have a general usage in the Community, especially among youths.

|  |  |
|---|---|
| Abstract me | Playing games with me |
| Beat yo down | To be physically beaten |
| Beef | Misunderstanding; disagreement |
| Bitch | Referring to any female besides relatives; female who snobs them |
| Bus toe | Any one that has Aids |
| Check it out | Observe it; investigate it, understand it |
| Cho | Not believing; disregarding |
| Chronic | Marijuana, weed |
| Cougar | Middle aged women who are divorced or separated and attracts younger male |
| Crack head | Person who is addicted to crack cocaine |
| Crank | Sexual intercourse |
| De bang | Is involved with illegal gang activities |
| Dis | Disrespect; not to be tolerated |
| Fiteque | Pressure brought on by Police during interrogation |
| Freak | Promiscuous young female |
| Fresh | New; popular; nice |
| General | The highest boss of the gang |
| Get d sense | Do you understand |
| Go an bad | Making noise; quarrelling; fighting, loud sexual behavior |
| Got yo bak | Support you or agree with you |
| Haul up | Come to the spot |
| Hold it down | Keeping things under control, not giving any trouble |
| Home bwoy | Affectionate male friend |
| Hood | Area where one lives; could be street corner or entire section of the City |
| Kool | Acceptable behavior |

| | |
|---|---|
| Mad stare | To stare someone with intent to fight or quarrel |
| My bwoy | Close friend but sometimes used to refer to any male (usually young) |
| My man | Close friend; but like previous term also refers to a male. In Belize, females sometimes refer to each other with this term. |
| Ova stand | Understand |
| Paro | To be high on drugs |
| Play out ya | Not taking things seriously |
| Punk | Male youth with unacceptable behavior |
| Roll up | Roll a weed |
| Rude bwoy | Street youth usually has had contact with the Police. |
| Sen an | Give me what's mine |
| Serious ting | Take it seriously |
| Sic up | Any one that has HIV |
| Simple | Easy to take advantage of |
| Sketel | Street female; party goer reflected in certain styles |
| Sprang | Out of control; crack cocaine addiction |
| Step pan yo | To be beaten |
| Stin an | Has mixed meaning. I.e., make your point, to bring pressure on someone |
| Strapped | Carrying a gun, usually hidden under clothing |
| Sugar daddy | Older man who shower younger female with money and jewellery, house, car, etc. |
| Sugar mama | Older women who showers younger male with money, jewellery, house, car etc. |
| Sweat yo | To be put under pressure |
| Tek wa packing | To be beaten |
| Train | Several male youths having forced intercourse with one female |
| Trip | Worrying, panicking |
| Violation | Breaking the rules of the accepted order |

# Abbreviations

| | |
|---|---|
| A.A. | Affirmative Action |
| B.D.O.C. | Belize Department of Corrections |
| B.F.L.A. | Belize Family Life Association |
| C.C.E. | Commission of Crime Eradication |
| C.C.Y.D. | CARICOM Commission on Youth Development |
| C.D.B. | Caribbean Development Bank |
| C.E.T. | Center for Employment Training |
| C.P.U.C. | Community Policing Unit Center |
| C.S.M.E. | Caribbean Single Market and Economy |
| C.Y.D.P. | Conscious Youth Development Program |
| D.C. | District Council |
| D.E.A | Drug Enforcement Administration |
| D.P.P. | Director of Public Prosecutions |
| DSM R III | Diagnostic and Statistical Manual of Mental Disorders |
| E.U. | European Union |
| F.A.R.C. | Armed Revolutionary Forces of Colombia |
| I.C.J. | International Court of Justice |
| I.D.B. | Inter-American Development Bank |
| I.R.A. | Irish Republican Army |
| I.T.V.E.T. | Institute for Technical Vocational Education and Training |
| J.L.P. | Jamaica Labor Party |
| K.H.M.H. | Karl Heusner Memorial Hospital |

| | |
|---|---|
| N.C.F.C. | National Committee for Families and Children |
| N.D.A.C.C. | National Drug Abuse Control Council |
| N.G.O. | Non-government Organization |
| N.I.C.H. | National Institute of Culture and History |
| N.O.P.C.A. | National Organization for the Prevention of Child Abuse |
| N.Y.C. | National Youth Council |
| N.Y.S.C. | National Youth Cadet Service Corps |
| O.P.E.C. | Organization of the Petroleum Exporting Countries |
| P.D. | Personality Disorder |
| P.N.P. | People's National Party |
| P.U.P. | People's United Party |
| U.B.A.D. | United Black Association for Development |
| U.D.P. | United Democratic Party |
| Y.C.D.C. | Yabra Citizens Development Committee |
| Y.E.A. | Youth Enhancement Academy |
| Y.F.F. | Youth for the Future |
| Y.G.U. | Youth Governance Unit |
| Y.M.C.A. | Young Men's Christian Association |
| Y.W.C.A. | Young Women's Christian Association |

# References

1. Hancock F. An Assessment of Juvenile Justice in Belize. Belize; 2000.

2. United States of America National Criminal Justice Commission. Real War on Crime: the Report of the National Criminal Justice Commission. Donziger SR, editor. New York: Harper Collins; 1996.

3. National Human Development Advisory Committee. From Boys to Men. Belize; 2001.

4. Jacobs PA, Baikie AG, Court Brown WM, MacGregor TN, Maclean N, Harnden DG. Evidence for the Existence of the Human "Super Female." Lancet. 1959;II.

5. Montagu A. Chromosomes and Crime. Psychol Today. 1968;II(5).

6. Law Revision Commissioner. Crime Control and Criminal Justice Act, Chapter 102. Belize; 2000.

7. Dostoyevsky F. The House of the Dead. St. Petersburg: Vremya; 1862.

8. Edwards C. Belizean Children in Especially Difficult Circumstances. Belize; 1994.

9. Gayle H, Hewlett M, Amaya A. Male Social Participation and Violence in Urban Belize. Belize; 2010.

10. Chinweizu I. Decolonising the African Mind. Ann Arbor: Pero Press; 1987.

11. Association American Psychiatric. Diagnostic and Statistical Manual of Mental Disorders: DSM-III-R. III. American Psychiatric In; 1987.

12. Headley B. A Spade is Still a Spade: Essays on Crime and The Politics of Jamaica. Austin: LMH Publishing Company; 2002.

# Index of Essays

# About The Author

Nuri Muhammad is a globally renowned and highly esteemed faith leader, social entrepreneur, political commentator and public servant. Youth advocacy has played a central and recurring role in his exemplary life of servant leadership. As his name (Nuri: light) suggests, he has been a brightly shining beacon of light beckoning the youth of Belize toward a future beyond gang culture, cyclical violence and social dysfunction. He has tirelessly advocated on behalf of the youth of Belize in multiple capacities including:

- First Director of The Youth Department (1993)
- Project Manager, National Youth Cadet Corps
- Director of Education and Rehabilitation, Belize Department of Corrections
- Coordinator, Conscious Youth Development Program (CYDP)
- Director, Youth Enhancement Agency (YEA)
- Executive Director, Youth for the Future

Nuri brings a global perspective to each endeavor he undertakes. He is able to seamlessly navigate cultural borders to find common ground and deliver outstanding results. A charismatic leader and true nationalist—Nuri has dedicated his adult life to empowering Belizeans, enriching and elevating the common discourse and finding solutions to the most pressing challenges the country faces.

Despite his many accomplishments, Nuri is most proud of his role as husband, father and integral founding member of the Belizean Muslim Community.

Contact the author (email): innadynamics@gmail.com

www.ingramcontent.com/pod-product-compliance
Lightning Source LLC
Chambersburg PA
CBHW051958090426
42741CB00008B/1447